Dearest Sid and Muriel,

It's been lovely exploring and sharing this 'human jungle' with you both.

Much love

Stan & Sue

London
June 1996.

Human
Jungle

Human Jungle

Stanton Newman

PROFESSOR OF PSYCHOLOGY, UNIVERSITY COLLEGE LONDON

and Susan Lonsdale

M. Phil (NATAL) M.Sc.(LSE)

Photography by Mark Jenkinson (USA)
and Stephen Lovell-Davis (UK)

Ebury Press

First published in 1996

1 3 5 7 9 10 8 6 4 2

Text copyright © 1996 Stanton Newman and Susan
Lonsdale
Based on the **Human Jungle** television series by
arrangement with **Wall to Wall Television Ltd**

First published in the United Kingdom in 1996 by
Ebury Press
Random House, 20 Vauxhall Bridge Road,
London SW1V 25A

Random House Australia (Pty) Limited
20 Alfred Street, Milsons Point, Sydney
New South Wales 2061, Australia

Random House New Zealand Limited
18 Poland Road, Glenfield
Auckland 10, New Zealand

Random House South Africa (Pty) Limited
PO Box 337, Bergvlei, South Africa

Random House UK Limited Reg. No. 954009

A catalogue record for this book is available from the
British Library

ISBN: 0 09 181389 1

Editors: Margot Richardson, Patricia Dunnett
Designer: Paul Welti

Printed and bound in Great Britain by
Butler and Tanner

Papers used by Ebury Press are natural recyclable
products made from wood grown in sustainable
forests

Contents

Acknowledgements

There are a great many people we would like to acknowledge for their contribution to this book, albeit often unwittingly. We would like to thank our friends who tolerated long silences, refusals to socialize and, we hope, only occasional grumpiness, as we relentlessly shut ourselves off to write to deadlines that could not be postponed, which we thought were impossible but which were finally made.

We also want to acknowledge all the hundreds of other writers whose ideas and thoughts inspired us as we sifted through many studies of urban life. As academic writers, we normally follow the convention of acknowledging each idea and theory developed, and each fact painstakingly accumulated, by others. But this book is not intended for other academics. It is for the general reader who shares our love and enthusiasm for the city with all its vigour and despite its faults. So, we have had to eschew this courtesy and hope we shall be forgiven for the wider audience the book will reach. We trust that those from whose work we have freely drawn will approve of the goal of achieving a wider currency for their work. We have included a list of further references for those readers who want to take these ideas just a little further.

Another rule of academic life which we had to leave behind was that of setting our own timetable. The development and testing of ideas which is the cornerstone of academic life has its own momentum. We were soon to discover that the schedule of a television series is not to be kept waiting, and our lives over the past few months have been dedicated to serving this new master, to producing a book to complement the series. In doing this we would like to thank the directors of the television series, Leanne Klein and Daniel Percivel, whose astute observations of the city and determined search for facts led us to firm up our own ideas of city life. Devising the scripts with them has been very satisfying and contributed considerably to the book's direction. We are full of admiration too for the passion and understanding demonstrated by the photographers, Mark Jenkinson and Steve Lovell-Davis. We would also like to thank all those involved with the project at Wall to Wall, especially Alex Graham and Patricia Dunnett for reading and commenting on the first draft of this book. Thanks also to Fiona MacIntyre and Margot Richardson at Ebury Press for their help and encouragement.

A large number of people have been very helpful and generous in sharing with us information from their own research. Without their help this book would be incomplete. We would like to thank them for their patience in trying to answer the probably unanswerable and obscure questions we would ask from time to time. Dennis Fabian, who along with his architectural colleagues fed us with literature and ideas, even when we interrupted their attempts to design even better cityscapes. John Gladstone who was always ready to tell us how animals other than humans would have behaved. Liz Wake was hugely helpful, not only in practical ways, but by always being forbearing and obliging. Ray Bradshaw of Nottingham University and Mike Atyeo from British Telecom were kind enough to send helpful information in a very short space of time.

Above all, we'd like to acknowledge *homo urbanus*, our eponymous hero or heroine, whose capacity to take on the challenge of the city, warts and all, we salute.

STANTON NEWMAN AND SUSAN LONSDALE

Chapter 1

Life at Speed

Being in the city inevitably has made me more motivated, more organized. You just have to be, especially when you have a child like I do, and a job and a school and a home and a secondary job as well to co-ordinate. But the thing about being in London, is that there's always something to stretch to.
ANASTASIA–London

The Global City Culture

In the past hundred years, the human habitat has changed more radically than ever before in the history of our species. We live in a world that our ancestors would barely recognize.

Human beings evolved in a world without skyscrapers or motor cars, in communities of hundreds not millions of others, in places where everyone knew the people around them and most would not travel beyond a 40km (25 mile) radius from the place they were born.

Yet the city is now the fastest growing habitat. The gradual drift of populations towards greater concentrations began in mid-nineteenth-century Europe with the Industrial Revolution, and has grown rapidly ever since. By the twenty-first century, more than half the world will live in cities. In some countries, the figure will be much greater. For instance, in 1950, nearly two-thirds of the population of the United States lived in urban areas. By 1990, this had already become three-quarters of the population. We are becoming an urban species.

People who inhabit cities have developed a new culture: that of *homo urbanus* or the urban human. These are people more at home in a city, regardless of where it is or what language is spoken, because they understand the general rules of how to deal with the city, its complexity and variety. They expect a high level of noise, a great number and variety of people, and enjoy the vast range of opportunities and the relatively fast pace of life offered to them there.

This is not to say that all cities are the same, but to argue that, across the world, they have something in common. So much so that people who live in cities share more with each other in terms of lifestyle and culture than they do with those who inhabit the countryside.

The urban environment is not always beneficial and there are aspects of city life that may be detrimental to our health, but *homo urbanus* has expectations and needs that can only be met by the diversity of life in the metropolis. The slow pace, peace and tranquillity of the countryside fills many city dwellers with alarm, representing as it does boredom and lassitude, monotony, conformity, lack of choice, and most importantly, the fear of being out of touch. It can only be sampled sporadically, if at all, for a short holiday or weekend away.

Highways speed people in and out of the city, day and night.

Adapting to city life The world is changing steadily such that city life will soon be the norm. How people live and cope in cities is an increasingly important question and one which we shall try to answer. The evolution of humans from a quiet, pastoral, and somewhat commodious life to the rush of the city with its cheek-by-jowl existence, noise, and information overload attests to the adaptability of the human organism.

Humans are more flexible than any other species. While most animals have a fairly fixed habitat, we can adapt ourselves to survive almost anywhere. We simply adjust our behaviour to suit the environment around us. The flexibility of individuals, their ability to adjust and accommodate to the demands of city life is the subject of this book.

ADAPTING TO DIFFERENT SITUATIONS

I think that [adapting] is something you have to do, because everything is happening so fast and so quickly . . . if you don't change, then something may happen to you. Not to say that it may be adverse, but . . . you need to keep on your toes. Let's say, for instance – a real minor example – the F train has a flood, you've got to get downtown, and you've got to find out how to get to the number four train . . . you've got to know how to get there. You do have to re-acclimatize yourself in these situations. I think the city forces you to.

PEPSI — New York

You have to change yourself, depending on personal relationships, work relationships, traffic relationships. You're always adapting here, which is kind of a good trait in someone .

ERROL — Los Angeles

The growth of the city

Moving through the city Urban conurbations have grown relative to rural areas. Sophisticated transport systems have enabled the size of cities to expand. With the separation of work and home, cities were limited by the distances people could cover to travel to and from work. We have moved from a walking and horse-drawn-carriage city to one which is determined by mass transit of rail and bus along with the car, and in some cases the aeroplane. In addition, the distribution of work by means of technology and communications has led to a dispersal of business and industry, further contributing to the expansion of the city.

Average commuting distances in the United States increased from about 14.5 to 18km (9 to 11 miles) between the 1970s and 1990s, and in the United Kingdom from about 8 to 14km (5 to 8 miles) between the 1960s and 1990s. Single-driver commuters also went up from about two-thirds to almost three-quarters during the 1980s. Although distances and single-driver commuting have both increased, average commuting times in the United States have not gone up. This has apparently been achieved by faster speeds, switching from slower buses to cars and away from the more congested peak-travel periods. Nonetheless, in the USA, the larger the city the longer the commuting time. Travel times for commuting in metropolitan areas with populations of less than 250,000 are approximately one-third less than commuting in metropolitan areas of 3 million or more. The situation in the United Kingdom, particularly London, is less clear. London attracts a large proportion of long-distance commuters who travel from towns and villages outside the city and use the good high speed train connections for their travel.

The development of information and communication technologies is leading to a movement of jobs away from central city locations. Some planners see the growth of telecommunications posing a threat to the single central city area, so that in the long term it will become obsolete.

Central to this view is the development of the mobile office or the telecommuter. Telecommuters do not need to go to a central point to conduct their work, but rely on telecommunications to do much of it from wherever they happen to be: home, car, even aeroplane. They quite literally construct a mobile office. Studies on telecommuters have shown they value the time flexibility that telecommuting makes possible, the reduction in commuting time and commuting stress. In addition, they report higher work satisfaction. On the economic side, productivity gains of up to 30 per cent have been found among telecommuters. The disadvantages of working this way usually fall on the employee and include the need to keep equipment at home and the space this takes, increased domestic costs such as heating and electricity, and the sceptical attitudes of some of their co-workers.

Cars in the city The association between cars and modern urban life is inescapable. The number of automobiles has risen from 127 million in 1960, to over 500 million in the 1990s. In fact, modern life may be considered a shrine to the motor car with ribbons of roads careering across the landscape of the country, and cities festooned with streets and the instruments of car control: traffic lights, parking meters, bollards, road markings and signs telling drivers what they may or may not do. The actual space covered by roads is remarkable. In Los Angeles, for instance, nearly a third of all land space is occupied by roads.

Above all, city life is epitomized by the rush-hour commute. Cars are tucked in bumper to bumper while they snake slowly into the city. Once there, they line the streets, are swallowed up by underground carparks, or are stacked high by multi-storey garages. Despite the fact that the average speed of the car in central London has declined to less than 24km (15 miles) per hour – slower than the horse and cart at the turn of the century – our love affair with the car continues.

Psychologically, the car remains attractive. It provides a semblance of control over our world. We are not tied to public transport which moves at somebody else's will. We can control our own starting and stopping. Or so we think . . .

Moving between cities Nothing epitomizes the development of a global culture of cities as much as the way in which travelling between cities has developed. Travel used to be a local affair dominated by the car, bus and train. Growth in air travel over the last thirty years, however, has been phenomenal. It has allowed people to keep in personal contact and bridge considerable geographic divides. While established relationships can be maintained by telecommunications, initial contacts often require a face-to-face meeting. Mass air travel makes this possible.

Air travel has moved from being the exception to the chosen mode of transport used by many in industrialized countries. Paid passenger travel increased more than threefold between 1970 and 1990. This growth was largely due to business travel where the increasing complexity of business puts pressure on the need for face-to-face meetings. As well, a not inconsiderable part of it was due to the rise of international tourism. Both were encouraged by the fall in real terms of the cost of travelling by air. Technological development has been an important feature in expanding passenger capacity and reducing the lengths of flights. In addition, airports and their terminals are now designed to carry large volumes of passengers.

Air travel has increased threefold over the last 20 years and is now more of a rule, rather than an exception.

The busiest airport in the world, Chicago O'Hare, deals with over 65 million passengers every year.

The traditional alternative, sea travel, has been relegated to transporting goods and for tourist cruises. Some cities lying on rivers have commuter river buses, such as the long-established boat for commuters between Nesodden and Oslo in Norway. More recently, a river bus has been re-introduced on the Thames in London. This type of transport is usually located within cities and is the exception rather than the rule.

High-speed railways have been developed as a realistic alternative to aeroplanes for inter-city travel in Japan and Europe, with trains travelling at speeds of over 200km (125 miles) per hour. In Japan, the relatively small distances between cities make train travel a viable alternative to air. Of inter-city trips between 500 and 750km (310 and 466 miles), over 70 per cent are done by rail, and only 14 per cent by air. As distances increase so the proportion of rail travel declines. Nonetheless, rail travel retains 40 per cent of trips between 750 and 1,000 km (466 and 620 miles), while air travel goes up to 46 per cent at this distance. Further developments in rail travel – such as the Chunnel train between England and France – are likely to make it more of a challenge to air travel.

Our heightened arousal in the city enables us to respond more quickly in certain situations.

The buzz of the city

Arousal Biologically, human beings are aroused by the amount of stimulation around them. States of arousal and non-arousal go from coma, sleep and drowsiness at one end, to animation, excitement, and exhilaration at the other. These states can be experienced either positively or negatively: for example, calmness or lethargy, exhilaration or panic.

The modern city is full of situations which trigger physiological arousal. The physiological changes that occur at times of arousal include increased flows of adrenaline (epinephrine). Dilatation of the peripheral blood vessels results in increased blood flow to the muscles. This allows for more rapid responses to stimuli. The heart rate goes up, increasing general blood flow. More blood is pumped to the brain, in particular the brain-stem and reticular formation which mediate arousal; it also appears to flow to other structures of the brain such as the limbic system which contributes to determining mood. The frontal brain lobes, which are intimately involved in attention and arousal, are

also thought to have increased blood flow (although this idea has become controversial). Overall, cerebral metabolism increases in times of arousal and so we are able to respond more quickly to stimuli.

Tunnel vision   When we walk through cities we are bombarded by stimuli of all types. Imagine walking into a busy street with the noise of cars, people and roadworks. The sounds may be unpleasant, but increase our arousal. When aroused, adrenalin pumps through our body, making us react more quickly than normal. Our heart rate increases the blood flow to our muscles enabling us, for example, to break quickly into a run to catch a bus. Our heightened arousal has meant we can react rapidly.

Although raised arousal may be useful, there is a limit to how much our senses can take in at once. For example, when we step off the train at a busy city station after the relative quiet of our journey, our senses are bombarded. There is simply too much noise, too many people, too much happening for our brain to process all of it. We're overloaded.

In 1987 a psychologist, Stanley Milgram, argued that when city dwellers experience information overload, it is dealt with by an attentional filtering process. In general, we appear to have a set amount of attention to allocate to stimuli in our world at any particular time. When something catches our attention or when the scene at our central point of vision is complex and demanding, we have less capacity to attend to the periphery. Increased arousal, however, helps overcome this and makes us more able to cope with all the stimuli around us. So the general level of arousal in the busy station may enable us to attend to more of the stimuli, but we still have to ignore some of what is going on as we do not have the capacity to deal with everything. It is as if we have tunnel vision. Some excellent studies have been performed in the laboratory to illustrate this process.

We appear to be particularly sensitive to certain stimuli. We have a low threshold, for instance, when it comes to the sound of our own name. Most of us are familiar with the experience of being able to hear our name mentioned, even across a noisy room full of people or the buzz of a cocktail party. We each have our own biases that affect those things we wish to hear or see and those we do not.

A number of studies suggest that when we walk down a busy city street full of sound and movement we filter out the stimuli to those appearing at our central point of vision, or to those which are important to us. This is a necessary response to over-stimulation and our limited capacity to pay attention to everything around us. We thus ignore certain things in

TUNNEL VISION

In one study, volunteers were given in their central vision a series of tasks which varied in complexity. While they were performing the task in central vision a stimulus was displayed in their peripheral vision. As the demands and complexity of the task in central vision increased they were less able to extract information from the peripheral stimulus. In addition, the further away the peripheral task was from central vision, the less they were able to process the information in the periphery.

Thriving in the fast lane, homo urbanus does many things at the same time.

A fast pace makes our lives feel busier, affording us goals and challenges, but also creating pressures.

the environment and may be seen to take them for granted. This applies in particular to things that regularly appear in the line of sight as we walk through the street. When homeless people first appeared on the streets of London, its citizens were shocked and concerned at the sight. After a number of years on the scene, it is now regularly taken for granted. Commuters on their way to work may not even notice, or filter out, the sight of young people who have been sleeping rough in the same spot for some time.

City life is made up of a huge number of encounters with potential sensory and information overload. Adapting to this by tunnelling our attention has been institutionalized into new rules of behaviour for the city. People don't stop and talk, they keep their faces blank and their eyes straight ahead. In so doing, they are not just protecting themselves, but avoiding overloading other people too.

There is a limit to how much we can attend to at the same time and at busy times such as walking fast to work, we will filter out all but the necessary sights and sounds.

Speed of city life The pace of our lives was once ruled by the rhythm of the sun and the changing seasons. But not any more. Speed has become part of the culture of the modern city. Compared to our ancestors we lead vastly accelerated lives.

It is often suggested that the pace of life in cities is faster than that in smaller towns and rural areas. Some studies have examined this by looking at how fast people do certain things in the city. Classic amongst these studies is a consideration of how fast people walk.

Walking in the city People in cities walk at about 1 to 1.6m (3 to 5ft) per second, considerably faster than people in small villages. This may seem paradoxical, but city dwellers have learnt to move very efficiently *en masse*; everyone co-operates to keep up with the pace. The density of crowds at the time of measurement is an obvious factor associated with how fast people are able to walk, but a remarkably consistent finding demonstrates that people walk faster in larger cities that they do in smaller ones. Studies in the United States, Britain, mainland Europe, Japan, Taiwan, Indonesia and Australia have all produced

It's a real fast pace . . . It's like every day is your last day in **New York**. Everybody's running around getting everything done, and you really get caught up in that. If you're sitting in your house not doing anything with your life or yourself you really get depressed in **New York**.

TANYA — New York

It's funny, 'cause where I grew up [in a small town] everyone worried about how far it was. They said, 'how many miles is it?' Out here, it's 'how much time does it take?' They don't care if you have to go 20 miles [32km] out of your way, but if you can save twenty minutes it's worth it. It's a much faster pace here; you have to plan your day. It's like you're never home. You have people calling you at home at 11, 12 o'clock at night. And you never get that fifteen to twenty minutes to yourself, to kick back and relax.

Everyone's in a hurry; everyone has to be some place. You worry about five minutes in time here. It's amazing how much time means out here, where back home they're a little more laid back. I don't know if that's a negative or a positive. It just depends on the individual.

DAVE — Los Angeles

I like to live very quickly. I like things to move fast. I like to wake up, have something to do as soon as I get up. I usually run late; part of me thinks I do that on purpose because I feel weird if I am running on time. If I'm not rushing, then I didn't do enough. I usually try and cram too many things in a day.

VERONICA — Los Angeles

The pace of London is much faster. I thrive on that, but it takes you too far sometimes – where you actually do too much, so you end up running for tubes that you don't need to run for, because there'll be another one coming along; whereas in **Cornwall** there's one bus a day, so you just kind of sit there.

ALEX — London

I try to keep upgrading myself to keep pace with city life. I have the advantage of having been in the bigger city and that sort of woke me up. I try and tell people [to] wake up before it's too late. Take that course or do something to get in tune. London is moving fast.

SAUNDRA — London

WALKING FAST

I wasn't used to it, being from a small city. You just go with the flow. What I've learned is that everyone's walking so fast, and even though I don't have some place to go I'm going to walk fast because they are. I think you just cope with it because everyone else around you is that way, and either you're going to get swallowed up or you go with it.

SHERRIE — New York

similar results. It is as if the larger the city, the greater the urgency, and hence the faster the walking speed. In addition, there are a number of other influences on walking speed, such as noise and pollution. The higher the levels of noise or pollution the faster people seem to walk.

Doing deals in the city Some researchers have looked at the way in which transactions occur, such as buying something from a shop. Comparisons between urban and rural settings show a similar difference to that of walking speed. Rural transactions not only take more time, but the increased time is often filled with more friendly behaviour. No doubt the friendly behaviour would be unhelpful to the city dweller with a busy agenda who is attempting to reduce their stimulation.

Both walking speed, and the speed of transactions like shop purchases, provide physical evidence that we do things more rapidly in cities. At a

Time has become a most valued commodity and is something we have a pressing need to manage. Air travel allows us to squeeze more into the time available.

THE TEMPO OF A CITY

Criteria used when making judgements regarding the tempo or pace of a city or town, in order of importance

HIGH AROUSAL/FAST PACE
1	Environment	crowded, noisy, traffic polluted, busy
2	Personal response	nervous, confusing, impatient
3	Time	hectic, urgent, rushed, stressed
4	Enjoyment/stimulation	lively, fun, exciting

LOW AROUSAL/SLOW PACE
1	Personal	relaxed, retired
2	Environmental	peaceful, laid back, parks quiet, easy-going
3	Time	patient and leisurely

(Adapted from Sadalla et al, *Environment & Behaviour*, March 1990)

psychological level, when people are asked whether a particular city is fast or slow, they are able to make a judgement about this. Their judgement of the tempo or pace of a city involves more than simply noting that things get done faster.

A study by Sadalla et al (see box, left) looked at how we make judgements about the pace of towns, cities or rural environments. We appear to consider a number of factors other than simply the speed with which certain transactions are completed. These factors reflect either high or low arousal. The complexity of these judgements suggests we use external cues, like the speed with which things are done as well as other aspects of the environment such as noise and traffic. We also use our own experiences, attitudes and feelings to describe the tempo or pace of the environment, often giving it human characteristics like 'tense' or 'sensitive'.

When people make judgements about tempo and pace they also reflect the size of the city. Larger cities are consistently rated as faster in tempo and pace than smaller cities.

We seem to have developed a new strategy for coping with the demands of the city. We simply do everything more quickly, so that we can process more in a shorter space of time.

Time in the city *Flexibility of modern time* No longer are we governed by the rising and setting of the sun; we can reschedule our lives in the way we want. The industrial age forced us to fit in with strict time scheduling of work activities because the very acts of work required joint action at a fixed place. Although the concept of a nine to five job, with armies of workers filing into factories and offices at a fixed time is still a part of life for the majority of people, for a growing number it is becoming a thing of the past. Throughout the European Community, the growth of part-time working is an ongoing and significant change in the pattern of employment. Flexitime is now common in many work environments; by 1993, 12 per cent of workers in the United Kingdom were on flexitime and 9 per cent were working a system of 'annual hours'.

Influence of technology on time Technology has the potential to free the modern worker from the shackles of time. It allows many people in the city to postpone, reorganize and reschedule their lives. Fax machines mean we are not reliant on the post and can demand instant responses. Being out of the office no longer means missing that important call because we either have answer machines or mobile telephones. We delay answering the telephone by using answer machines. Despite initial consumer resistance, these are now an integral part of city life. The video recorder liberates us from the constraints of television programmers. Shopping can now be done in most cities at any time of the day or night, either by mail-order or in person .

In addition, technology has the ability to increase our leisure time, (but not necessarily the resources to fill that time). Working hours in many industrial countries fell dramatically from the 1960s until the 1980s when the fall stopped. Despite this, it is interesting to note that surveys of employees' attitudes in the USA show that one-third of working people would sacrifice some income to work shorter hours. A pressing need in many families is perceived to be more 'quality time' with each other. Technology may not yet have reduced working time sufficiently for those in work, but its potential to do so remains.

Surprisingly, the returns expected from technology have not yet fully materialized. New technology can sometimes create a time pressure of its own, as it gives us a sense of always being available to respond immediately. One aspect of this is that modern technology means we can be on the job twenty-four hours a day. The division between work time and leisure time becomes less clear. The mobile phone and fax can find us wherever we are and have created an expectation that we will always be available. We even

RESCHEDULING

Sometimes I can put off going to the pharmacy or going to the market until two o'clock in the morning. I have done my shopping at 2 am because I just couldn't do it during the day.

VERONICA – Los Angeles

AVERAGE WORKING HOURS IN JAPAN, USA & UK, 1960-1990				
Year	1960	1970	1980	1990
Japan	2440	2220	2100	2095
USA	1975	1920	1800	1810
UK	2080	1890	1690	n. a.

(From ETUC, *Demos* 5/95)

use the time that we have available for leisure to remain in contact with our work by mobile communications. This should not necessarily be seen as a problem; the other side of the coin of increased availability is the flexibility to determine when that accessibility is actuated. The rules, as always, are in the hands of the machine-operators, not the machine itself.

Urgency of time We have built up a host of expectations about being able to obtain rapid responses from the others and the machinery that surrounds us. For example, our impatience grows when the computer we are working on does not respond within the number of seconds that we have grown accustomed to. Computer software designers know that we will require faster and faster responses from our machines, so shaving a few nanoseconds off the speed of a computer response has become the way to sell programmes.

It has been argued that time urgency is the toxic element of our society. The argument runs as follows: in studies of urban American cities the pace of life has been assessed using a variety of indicators. These include walking speed, talking speed, bank-teller speed, work speed and clock-watching. When these are put together, the faster the pace of life the higher the death rates from coronary heart disease. However, this needs to be set against many other factors thought to influence coronary heart disease, such as diet and exercise.

Pressure of time The increased speed required to do things – time urgency – must be distinguished from time pressure: the need to find more time to fit in all we have to do.

Time has become a most valued commodity and is something we have a pressing need to manage. One of the biggest complaints of people in the modern age is the sense that they do not have enough time to complete their activities. A study in the UK showed that one-quarter of British workers feel that they have too much to do. An illustration of the extent to which time pressure has significantly changed our behaviour is the finding that British working men sleep half an hour less now than they did thirty years ago.

TIME PRESSURE

There never seems to be enough hours in the day to do everything that you'd like to do, or need to do.

BETTY – Los Angeles

What stresses me about my life? Not having enough time in the day to do everything I need to get done. Something that would seem small, like going to a friend's house or going to the store or the dry cleaner, can take you a lot longer than you planned, just because of the traffic or the people, the amount of people trying to do the same thing.

VERONICA – Los Angeles

I feel like I'm wasting precious time when I'm not doing something that I could be doing to make me money or keep in touch with an acquaintance. There's so many things to do; so little time.

JUDY — New York

We have responded to time pressure by adopting a mode of behaviour which makes the time we do have at our disposal more intense. Even in our leisure time we try to compress things into smaller bursts. Instead of taking long slow walks for exercise we go to a quick aerobics class. In order not to waste time we try to do many things at the same time. We read and listen to a personal stereo while commuting. We drive and talk on a mobile phone at the same time. We channel-surf to watch more than one television programme. All these activities increase the intensity of our experience. They make our lives feel busier and give us the impression that the pace of life is getting faster still.

Enjoying the fast lane Not everyone wants to slow down and have more leisure time. Over two-thirds of people who are asked if they would continue to work even if they had no financial need, say they would remain in work.

For the majority of people, retirement brings untold time for leisure, but many have difficulty in slowing down with no deadlines or objectives to meet. While the work

SLEEP

I never seem to have enough time in the day. I only sleep maybe three hours a night. The only time I have free is from eleven o'clock to about two in the morning when I go to sleep, and then I have to be up again at five, five-thirty to get to work on time. I don't like to sleep a lot but I wish I had a couple of more hours to do that. Maybe I wouldn't be so tired.

DAVE – Los Angeles

I've managed to get by on a lot less sleep. Eight hours' sleep a night would be a luxury for me. And that doesn't mean I don't want it once in a while, but typically, five or six hours a night has become normal. Add it up in a week, I've got hour for hour just a lot more up-time.

RICHARD – New York

DOING LOTS OF THINGS AT ONCE

As you're working, you have to not only be on the phone but while you're on the phone, you've got to save time by looking through some résumés; you've got to save time by working on the computer. And as you're listening to a person, putting them on the headsets, mute, so that you can talk to someone else as you're listening to this person. So you're doing lots of things at one time.

DAVE – Los Angeles

When I'm driving I need to be smoking a cigarette, adjusting the mirrors, changing the radio stations, drinking a beverage, perhaps talking on the phone, communicating with other drivers. When I'm watching television, I need to be painting my nails or reading a magazine. It's hard for me to focus on just one thing unless it's really absorbing, like a book.

MARY – New York

I've got the art of reading my newspaper, eating my dinner and actually driving at the same time. I can do that quite easily. I think city life allows you to do that. I mean, you have to do that just to survive.

PINKY – London

BOREDOM WITH NOTHING TO DO AND DIFFICULTY SLOWING DOWN

It's funny: when you take a day off of work, for one day it's great, but in two days it gets real slow. You start thinking 'what can I do?' I'm always trying to think of things to keep me busy, especially when there's nobody else around. I need people around. I need people to talk to all the time. Being in a city breeds you that way.

DAVE – Los Angeles

I'm a high energy type person, so if I'm stopped and it's not by will, like somebody else, like traffic or an elevator, that is just really frustrating. I don't like, flip out, screaming and like, but just somebody else having control over my situation and me losing control over it, I really don't like that at all. So I like to have absolute control over the situation.

SHELLY – New York

SLOWING DOWN CAUSING STRESS

I do lose it. Most of the time that would be in the car driving in traffic. There's very few things that can set me off. I can deal with a lot, I think you have to live here. But one of the things where I do lose it is in a car in traffic when I'm counting on being somewhere at some point and that's being prevented. It's that period of being out of control of the situation that drives me nuts.

RICHARD – New York

Driving. I think you get stuck on the freeway wondering why its 55 miles an hour and you're not even going 5. And you're wondering well, does that mean that the times when you can go 55 can you go 90 because you want to average it out. You don't want to be stopped, you don't understand why you're stopped, you can't understand why you're not going 60 miles an hour on the freeway, that drives you nuts.

DAVE – Los Angeles

role provides a range of intangible benefits, such as a position and status in society as well as social contacts, it also gives us goals and challenges despite – or perhaps because of – the pressures involved.

For many busy city dwellers, a summer holiday of about two or even three weeks is about as much as we can deal with. The absence of structure and purpose is unsettling and the lack of the challenge of work makes leisure less satisfying. Far from being a negative experience, work is indeed stimulating and pleasurable. When people are asked to rank what they enjoy doing, seeing family and friends are placed first and work activities second – even above leisure activities such as watching television or playing sport.

A dramatic illustration of the problems of excess leisure is shown in a study of elderly people in Finland. Its purpose was to identify what factors predicted both life satisfaction and mortality following retirement. Amongst a number of factors shown to predict poor life satisfaction and increased levels of mortality was excessive leisure time. Having too much time for leisure can be dangerous to your health.

In order to overcome the psychological stress of being impeded by other traffic, many people are taking to the bicycle as a quick means of getting around the city.

City stress

A number of features of city life are thought to be stressful: noise, speed, and crowding are some of them. However, each of these apparently troublesome characteristics has its corollary, such as being invigorating, convenient and offering choice.

What interests us is how *homo urbanus* deals with the former, while reaching out for the gains to be found in the latter.

Traffic stress Many people assume that driving *per se* is stressful. Our adaptation to a life at speed means we expect to move fast. Real physiological stress, however, occurs not simply from driving or commuting, but when those journeys are impeded.

There is a distinction between objective and subjective impediments: that is, actual obstructions when driving and our perceptions of how much we are obstructed. The latter to some extent depends on our expectations of how quickly we should travel from one point to another. It is how much we *think* we are being obstructed or held up more than how much we *are* held up that creates stress. Perhaps surprisingly, subjective perceptions do not always directly correspond to actual physical impediments. However, they do influence the effect on us of actual physical obstructions. They in turn are affected by our general mood. In a study of mood at home or in general, the extent of subjectively perceived impediments to commuting was directly related to low mood.

Driving in itself is not necessarily stressful. Traffic stress arises when our journeys are impeded. Traffic jams cause frustration because we lose our sense of control over the car and the road.

In Los Angeles, the most stressful thing for me is being in my car. Oh, it's like a nightmare. I love to drive my car. It's a very fast car, a powerful piece of machinery and when I get in it I want to go. I don't want to drive five miles [8km] an hour behind a bus breathing pollution.

KENYA – Los Angeles

If I set out timely to do something and I'm in a traffic jam for two hours, yeah, that annoys me and then I start really wanting to punch somebody.

SAUNDRA – London

I was stuck in traffic, my car was overheating, it was the middle of summer, and it started to sprinkle, it was really freaky weather, and on the talk radio I couldn't get a good station, so I ended up just pulling off the knobs on my radio and throwing them out the window.

KATH — Los Angeles

It's the people who waddle in front of you slowly and are completely unaware of the fact that they're in a crowd and that they should be aware, not just of where they're going, but how they're taking up space on a thoroughfare. People who pause to have conversations in the middle of a sidewalk instead of moving on. Those are the people that drive me crazy.
I've been out, and I come over the bridge and there's a wall of traffic and it's there because of a construction project, and it's delaying me from getting home. You anticipate that ride being fifteen minutes; suddenly it's double or triple that. And that's what drives me nuts.

RICHARD – New York

One of the reasons we tend to try and find short cuts is not that they actually reduce journey time. It is rather that they tend to give us the feeling that we are making progress and avoiding being impeded.

One group of people who drive for a living – bus drivers – have been well analysed. The stress associated with the job of a bus driver has also been shown to be directly related to the amount of peak hour traffic that they have to negotiate. It is also related to the degree of control drivers feel they have over their job: the more control, the less the stress.

City dwellers are, therefore, faced with the conundrum that they need mass transport systems but know that occupations such as bus driving can be stressful. One alternative might be to introduce trams so that cars have to give way to mass transport rather than hapless bus drivers negotiating their way around cars, especially in peak hour traffic. Another alternative might be to look at ways of giving bus drivers more control.

Delays at airports have much the same result as delays or impediments to motor cars. Many people find plane travel stressful. It appears that it is particularly stressful for those passengers who are delayed. It is simple to compare expected and actual times of departure of flights, and studies show that people who are delayed on take-off are more agitated than those who are not delayed. Their frustration spills over into their general attitudes and they tend to blame the particular airline they were flying at the time. The result is that delayed passengers give a lower evaluation of overall airline performance.

The more control we have over our situation the less stress we feel. Whether it's sitting in traffic or waiting for a lift, a sense of predictability and control are key to whether we experience stress.

Noise stress Another source of stress is noise. Again, a distinction needs to be drawn between noise objectively measured and loudness subjectively felt. The level or intensity of noise objectively measured in decibels is not a clear predictor of the subjective judgement of loudness. Loudness is the subjective judgement we make in rating the level of noise.

The attitudes and beliefs we hold about the source of the noise seem to be critically important. A classic study found that ratings of loudness were higher when people were told the car noise they were hearing came from a teenager's hot rod, in comparison to their ratings when they were

TAKING SHORT CUTS, RAT RUNNING

When I'm driving on the freeway I feel like I'm a rat stuck in a maze, or as though I'm running on a treadmill. When I get somewhere on the side streets I feel like I beat the system somehow; like I did my own individual thing – and that makes me feel good.

KATH – Los Angeles

It makes me feel as though I'm getting there faster. At least I'm trying to do something about it. I've got to try. I think I'd be annoyed if I just sat there and took it. You have to be in control of the traffic jam or you've got to try and get out of it.

KHALID – London

told the noise came from a taxi. Besides the source of noise altering our perception of loudness, our beliefs and fears can also influence the degree to which a noise is judged as annoying. Studies of reactions to aircraft noise, for example, demonstrate that people who are most worried about aircraft crashes are the ones most unsettled by aircraft noise. Aggravation may increase with a rise in noise but the level of annoyance is influenced by beliefs and judgements. Studies on traffic noise show that higher levels of aggravation are associated with judging the road as dangerous, having problems with neighbours and when the land is used for both residential and commercial purposes. One interesting aspect of research on the effect of traffic noise is that younger people are more worried by a given level of noise, and this appears to be due to the fact that they hear better than older people.

Not all noise is annoying. It depends on the context. A high noise level at a rock concert contributes to our sense of excitement and enjoyment if we are in the audience. A similar level of noise from a neighbour's home is likely to fill us with irritation and alarm and cause us to become agitated.

What is important is that we have developed techniques of dealing with the noise of the city. A common phenomenon is the process of habituation to noise. When we experience a constant level of background noise, as we do in most cities, we tend to habituate to it such that we hardly notice it at all. Noise levels in a busy office, for example, are very high. But the workers tend to adapt to the noise level and no longer even consider it loud.

We tend to notice the absence of the noise if it suddenly goes away. We tend to be able to adapt to this constant noise, but it does take time.

NOISE

You learn to live with it. I've lived on a busy city street, and we just had to block out the noise. You have to stay focused on what you're doing. And that's the kind of concept of being in a big city. You have to focus everyone out of your ballpark and just focus on what you're doing at the time

DAVE – Los Angeles

I go right where I know a lot of people are, and I sit there and meditate. I'm used to a lot of noise, so I know how to block people out. They really don't interfere with me. But if it was quiet, then I'd be so alert and I wouldn't be able to concentrate, I wouldn't be able to drift inside of myself.

JODIE – Los Angeles

For Thanksgiving we went to the Catskills, the mountains in upstate New York. The house was up in the mountains, and there was no other house near it. It was absolutely silent, and I couldn't sleep. I had to take some medicine so I could sleep, because I was so used to hearing people outside or the noises. . . It's kind of ironic when you can't sleep without noise, but I think that in New York it becomes a sedative.

CLIFTON – New York

Dealing with stress

How different is *homo urbanus?* City dwellers appear to be subject to a life of greater speed and stimulation than people who live in the country. Whether city dwellers have grown to be able to deal with stresses any better than people from the country is still an open question: the expectations of city dwellers to be able to do things quickly may make them less tolerant of delays and stresses.

In a study which examined the cardiovascular response to a particular stress separate groups of city and country dwellers were assessed on standard stress. Their systolic blood pressure (SBP), diastolic blood pressure (DBP) and heart rate (HR) were measured. City dwellers had significantly higher SBP increments to stress than country dwellers. The authors of this study concluded that city life increases the physiological reactivity, the increase in blood pressure, of city dwellers when faced with stressing stimuli as compared to country dwellers. The question arises of whether city life leads to a different physiological state.

Psychological models of stress suggest that people adopt various strategies in an attempt to deal with stress. They first tend to evaluate the potential source of stress and then plan a strategy to deal with it. But societies differ in how they deal with general pressures of the city. In some societies the common response is to grin and bear it, ignore the stress as much as possible while in others the model is to confront and try and change the source of the stress. What is special about the stress of the city is that much of it is difficult to change, or will only change by the introduction of major planning changes which regulate the kinds of behaviours that take place in areas of the city. As a consequence, the main changes that have developed have been psychological changes within us, the city dweller. We have learned to adopt blocking techniques to the over stimulation, and we have learned to move fast to reduce the possibility of too many contacts.

The city bombards us with information and stimulation, forcing us to operate more quickly. The result is that we live at a faster pace than ever before. And yet we have adapted to this life with considerable skill. We have learnt new kinds of behaviour, become new kinds of people. But this process is not a static one. As we change and adapt, we change the environment around us too. We are part of a complete system: the city changes with us in an ever-evolving process.

In the city we live lives of greater speed and stimulation than ever before. **Homo urbanus has adapted to this life with considerable skill, learning new behaviour and becoming a new type of person.**

BLOCKING STIMULI OUT

When I first moved to London, I was taking everything in, too much in almost. Now I block certain things out, just to be able to have a calmer life.

ALEX – London

Chapter 2

Crowds and Space

Your guard's up all the time anyway, but it sort of intensifies when there are people right on you. Maybe in some respects you're a little bit more tolerant of that space being violated, because you get used to it compared to some-one that's not in the city. It doesn't mean it doesn't make you feel uncomfortable, but you have to deal with it: it's a fact of life living here, so get used to it.
RICHARD – New York

Instead of being evenly spread across the earth, individuals tend to cluster in large urban environments often in high rise flats or apartments.

Never before in the history of our species have so many people lived on such small spaces of land. And still the human population is growing at a dramatic rate. The population has doubled in the last forty years and is estimated to be about 5.5 billion. One estimate puts the daily excess of births over deaths at 200,000. The world population increases at the rate of a small town every day. In the space of a year this means hypothetically twenty-four additional cities of 3 million are created. It is predicted that by the year 2025 the population will be between 8 and 9 billion.

Population growth has been coupled with a dramatic increase in urbanization. Instead of being evenly spread across the earth, individuals have tended to cluster together in large urban environments. Three-quarters of the population of the United States now live in an urban milieu with the result that approximately 70 per cent of the population occupy 3 per cent of the land. In the developing world, rates of urbanization and population growth are both higher than in the developed world. In China, until recently a largely rural society, official figures state that 25 per cent of the population (300 million) now live in cities.

The net effect of these two forces, population growth and urbanization, has been to place enormous pressures on space. Some of the most densely populated 'countries' in the world have relatively small populations. For example, Monaco has a density of about 16,000 people per sq km (41,500 people per sq mile). Of the larger countries, Bangladesh has the greatest population density with about 838 people per sq km (2,170 people per sq mile). This compares with densities of approximately 238 per sq km (617 per sq mile) in the United Kingdom and 28 per sq km (72 per sq mile) in the USA.

Population and density in big cities

There is little dispute that the most populated city in the world is Tokyo, with a population of nearly 29 million. Mexico City with 23 million and Sao Paulo with 21 million are the next most populous cities. Overall, over 130 cities in the world now have a population of over 1 million. What is also important is that some cities attract large numbers of visitors and this serves to swell both the population of the city as well as its density. London, for example, attracts about 23 million visitors per year. Assuming an even spread of visitors throughout the year and that the average stay is five days then the city increases by over 300,000 per day. Clearly, tourism is not evenly spread over the year so on some days London's population may increase by half a million.

The impact of urbanization of Western industrial cities pales into insignificance in contrast to the big cities of the developing world. For example, the population of Mexico City increases by 1 million people annually and includes one-fifth of all Mexicans. It has half of all the national industries, and produces half of the national income of Mexico. In Beijing, the population of more than 9 million people uses 300,000 motor vehicles (including 4,000 buses) and 5.5 million bicycles. An enormous number of bicycles is now characteristic of a number of cities in developing countries of which Beijing is one and Delhi and Calcutta are others.

Size of a city is, however, only a part of the pressures of urban life. The density of cities does not show a simple relationship to size. The most densely populated cities with densities of over 38,600 per sq km (100,000 per sq mile) include Hong Kong, Bombay (India), Jakarta (Indonesia), Lagos (Nigeria), Shenyang (China) and Ho Chi Minh City (Vietnam).

Crowded cities There are considerable variations in our ability to adapt to density. In part this is defined culturally, and can be seen in planning regulations which specify the amount of space required for each person in residential buildings. Requirements in the USA are twice those that tend to be laid down in Europe, and European levels are about four times those found in Hong Kong.

The need to take account of cultural differences in an attempt to understand the relationship between density and psychological well-being emphasizes the importance of the beliefs people hold and the influence these have when they assess the impact of density. This brings us to the distinction between density and crowding, and the different judgements people make about the negative or positive consequences for them of having lots of people around.

Being near others Social density is an objective measure of the number of people in a specified area, whereas crowding is the subjective judgement of how dense certain environments are. Therefore, crowding is a psychological perception of a large throng of people while density is a physical measure of numbers of people.

The assessment of crowding does not always correspond to actual measures of density. This is an important finding because it means that it is not simply physical factors which determine our judgement of certain things. One important influential factor is the context in which we make that judgement. We will make a different assessment of crowding in an enclosed space than we would in an open space, such as a park, which will have nothing to do with the actual level of density.

There also appears to be a temporal aspect to judgements of crowding in which we are influenced by the length of time we have been in an area. Long-term residents in an area have been found to perceive their residential environment as less crowded than short term residents, suggesting that a process of adaptation has taken place. This adaptation changes people's perceptions of particular environments.

When we experience throngs of people as excessive and unpleasant, it has less to do with actual levels of density or numbers of people than with having our customary expectations breached. We find shopping centres unbearable, for instance, if there are more shoppers than we had expected and for which we had not prepared ourselves. We expect a greater number of shoppers at Christmas time and gird our loins accordingly. For some, the Christmas crowds signify a happy occasion and are part of the enjoyment of the season. For others, the increase in the number of shoppers is experienced as crowding. To someone from a small town who is used to a low density of people when shopping, coming to the big city for the first time with its crowds on normal shopping days can be an unnerving crowded experience. Coming back again and again, expectations are likely to be adjusted, and subsequently, the crowds may well be experienced as exciting and eventful.

Density and crowding in homes When people evaluate their satisfaction with a residential area, research suggests they tend to do this on three general dimensions. The first and most important is the judgement of space, the second is of people, and the third of services. The features that make up the first dimension include all aspects of the physical environment such as the balance of built-up and open spaces, the width of streets and, importantly, feelings of being crowded.

Evidence suggests that crowding in public places is less important to individuals' feelings of well-being than crowding at home. People who feel high levels of crowding at home usually also face actual restrictions in the space accessible to them as well as access to resources and facilities. This naturally limits the number of choices available to them and interferes in what they are able to do. It may also make adaptation more difficult.

Living in a block of flats with others above and below epitomizes life in the centre of the city. Although people living in flats or apartments are more likely to complain of loneliness, research indicates they have as many friends and social contacts as those living in houses. They also complain more about a lack of privacy. It appears that the inability to regulate and control the social interaction in large blocks of apartments is the real problem. If they venture into the public areas of the block they meet and are forced to interact with people with whom they may not want to spend time. This leads them to retreat into their apartments more often and then feel lonely. The different forces which may be at work with regard to interacting with neighbours in an apartment block and in a suburban street are quite complex and there is a need for more research to unravel these.

The high-rise flat or apartment has become a watchword in city residential developments. Again, there are cultural differences in the way residents perceive the high-rise apartment. In Britain, the high-rise building tends to have a negative association. It is unlikely to be the height itself which is somehow seen as unnatural. In many other cities, such as New York, Tel Aviv and Hong Kong, the higher up the apartment, the better the view and the more desirable and costly it becomes.

One study in Britain found that the dissatisfaction expressed by some residents of high-rise apartments was explained simply by their desire for a low-level dwelling and not any specific dislike of their high-rise apartment. These findings emphasize that the cultural norm in some countries is to have a low-rise dwelling and it is this predilection rather than something inherently bad that creates the attitudes prevalent in those societies towards high-rise buildings.

In wealthy areas the high-rise apartment may well be regarded as a luxurious place to live, where views are good and neighbours are individuals with high status. In poor neighbourhoods the standing of high-rise buildings is one which epitomizes poorly maintained public housing with graffiti, dirt and potential danger. Our images of high-rise residences, which influence our feelings of well being are largely determined by the quality of the neighbourhood, rather than height itself.

Out and about in the city Climate plays an important part in the use of public space. Areas used in the summer months by groups who congregate to take part in joint activities change dramatically according to the temperature. Winter use of plazas and other open spaces in cities is low, except where they are used for specific winter sports such as ice-skating on the Rockefeller Plaza in New York.

Urbanisation has put huge pressures on space and has led to dense and crowded living environments.

As the density of a space reduces, people use it differently. They deal with the cold by activities which keep them warm and engage in the odd sport of sun-following. People sitting in open spaces can be seen to chase the sun across the square. We also choose to go where other people are. Attempts to counteract the impact of cold on the use of public spaces has been to develop enclosed environments where people can congregate in warmth. The development of underground shopping malls in some northern cities has created large urban public spaces unaffected by the outside climate – again a testament to the ability of humans to adapt and for *homo urbanus* to create a lifestyle that, unlike that of our rural forebears, is not subject to the vagaries of the weather.

The perception of crowding in public places is not simply related to actual density but to the previous experience and expectations that people have of that public place. In winter, the expectation may be of low density; in summer of high density. If someone wishes to be private, they are unlikely to visit a city park in summer but they may do so in winter. Some people who live in the locality of a park may feel it is part of their personal neighbourhood and they tend to feel more crowded when 'their' park is invaded by others.

The purpose for which people wish to use the public space will also influence their perception of how crowded it is. In general, public areas only feel crowded when the density is beyond that expected and when it interferes with the objectives that the individual has in visiting it. The idea that a place is crowded, therefore, reflects a sense of unpredictability, 'it is more crowded than I expected', and lack of control, 'I cannot do what I set out to do'.

Another influence on our perception of whether a public place is crowded or not is whether we go there as part of a large or small group. Research suggests that someone who goes to a high-density city park as part of a large group will feel less crowded than if they go as part of a small group. Two reasons have been put forward for this finding. First, a large group may be more able to establish its own territory in the park and thus provide a protective cocoon to individual members. Second, individuals within a large group may be more prepared for a high number of interactions, so finding the area highly populated may not cause any discomfort.

People are enormously adaptive in dealing with situations they perceive to be too crowded. When they find a situation to be more crowded than they expected, for instance, people tend to adopt a course of action which enables them to adjust to it. One obvious response is to abandon the visit. More frequently, however, people either modify their expectations or change their objectives, allowing themselves to view that particular public place differently. This in turn leads to a reduction in their perception of the extent of crowding. In psychological terms, what this does is enable them to reassert their feelings of control and predictability. Many city dwellers are able to use this form of successful coping with instances of crowding. The long-term impact of this adaptive behaviour is that on future visits expectations will have shifted. However, not all city dwellers may be able to successfully deal with crowds in this way.

Feeling part of the crowd People also accept high levels of crowding in certain environments. Not all crowds are bad. Some environments require the active participation of many people to complete the event. Rock concerts and football matches all require large numbers of people to create the atmosphere and excitement. People are very happy in these situations to be packed cheek by jowl, and even though they would describe it as crowded they do not dislike it. Crowds are an intimate part of the process and the absence of a crowd would make the event less enjoyable.

Where individuals are brought together for a common purpose, or in the case of football two groups for competing purposes, the crowd provides a sense of identity and raises the level of emotions and excitement which together contribute to the enjoyment of the event.

The ritual behaviours of sports crowds place expectations on the individual in the crowd, getting them to participate in behaviours that they otherwise would not do. In fact many of the behaviours (ritual singing, Mexican waves) only make sense when done as a group. Crowds at sporting events set up temporary group norms for the period of activity, which place expectations upon the individuals in the crowd. These norms are dependent upon the group composition and purpose. Where two teams are in opposition the group behaviour is more likely to be aggressive and demonstrative, sometimes directed towards the opposing group of fans rather than towards the field of play. Where the allegiances are less defined, such as in many tennis matches, all the emotion is directed towards the actors on the court. The emotions at many of these events is contagious, such that the excitement of everybody is raised by hearing and seeing others express their excitement.

Disliking crowds Studies indicate that feeling crowded can have a number of negative effects. These can be observed at the physiological level by a measure known as the Galvanic Skin Response, a gauge of anxiety and discomfort which goes up when individuals feel crowded. It can also be observed in work situations when performance deteriorates, and psychologically, people report discomfort when they feel crowded. Interestingly, in the long term people appear less likely to form friendships with those that they have met in situations of overcrowding.

Movement in crowds

Negotiating street space Modern humans have an acute sense of the space around them – essential if they are to avoid collisions with strangers. At busy New York city intersections, more than 50,000 people will pass through in the space of one hour.

The exact number of pedestrians passing through an area is highly dependent on where the street is and what functions it performs: that is, the services and shops in the street, or where it leads. However, other influences on pedestrian shopping flows are the time of year, the day of the week, what time of day it is, and the weather.

Some detailed studies of pedestrian flow using time-lapsed photography have been undertaken by Ray Bradshaw in the main shopping area in the City of Nottingham, England. He found a remarkable difference in pedestrian flows between September and December. As might be expected, these reflected the increase at Christmas time. Some areas had pedestrian flows which increased up to five fold between September and December. One of the shopping streets generated flows of over 15,000 people per hour and occasionally went up to 22,000 people per hour during shopping times.

In addition to the time of the year, an important determinant of pedestrian flows is what day of the week it is. Saturday still reigns supreme, at least in Nottingham, but probably also elsewhere, as the day to shop. In September, Saturday had over one and a half times as many shoppers as a Wednesday, and in the run up to Christmas, Saturday had twice the number of shoppers.

Rain and snow keep people off the streets. Cities with inclement weather and lots of snow, such as some of the big Canadian cities, have responded by building large underground malls which function the year round.

Shopping flows differ from commuting flows in that with shopping flows there is much movement in opposite directions. Some shoppers begin at one end of the street while others do the reverse. In contrast, much pedestrian flow during rush hours is in the similar direction with flows from transport points towards office buildings.

The speed of walking in city streets ranges between about 60 and 107m (200 and 350ft) per minute. Given the density of urban environments, it is remarkable that more collisions don't take place. Walking in the streets is governed by a series of implicit rules which cover issues like how far apart to keep and who gives way to whom, etc. We do know that pedestrians when walking in an urban environment continually scan the pavement, normally walking at a slight angle to the pedestrian in front in

The exact number of pedestrians passing through an area is dependent on the street, its function, where it leads, the time of the year, week and day, as well as the weather.

order to gain a maximum view ahead. They also continually make small adjustments in their speed to avoid collisions: here speeding up to pass ahead of someone, then slowing down to let someone cross ahead. When two people approach each other from opposite directions, small deviations often accompanied by gestures or glances signal who will give way and in which direction a person will move. The signals and adjustments follow split-second decisions while travelling down a noisy and busy street, full of movement and colour. It shows the remarkable skills we have learned to be able to walk in densely packed streets.

For a pedestrian used to walking in a city, there are times when the pavement or sidewalk becomes most difficult to negotiate. This normally occurs in those cities which are popular with tourists. Tourists often stroll rather than walk, are not under any time pressure and are involved in looking at the city rather than walking through it with a purpose. As a result, they tend to disrupt the flow of walking for the city pedestrian on home territory. City dwellers also take holidays, however, and can adopt all the mannerisms of a tourist in their walk when they are on holiday, or at times even during their lunch break. The most purposeful walking on city pavements takes place when people share a similar objective: getting to and from work. In rush hours, people move in blocks purposefully tracking down the office, bus stop or train station, all wanting to move as quickly as possible.

A number of studies have looked at the behaviour of pedestrians as they move about shopping malls. Shopping malls are particularly interesting because walking is more open and unstructured, instead of being constrained and directed by instructions such as pedestrian crossing signals. Nonetheless, the unspoken rules that govern the pedestrian are brought into play and are implicitly understood by shoppers.

Thousands of pedestrians pass through this busy New York intersection every hour. Each pedestrian follows implicit rules of walking and makes a number of small adjustments to their speed to avoid collisions.

The rules of who gives way to whom not only provide an important mechanism to smooth the passage of people through shopping malls but offer an interesting insight into society. These studies found, in both the United States and the United Kingdom, that men tend to give way to women, showing the importance of residual social norms governing relations between the sexes. People who are able-bodied tend to give way to those with a disability. At the level of groups, relative power seems to be the rule governing who gives way. Smaller groups tend to be displaced by larger groups.

An interesting contrast between the United States and the United Kingdom was found in relation to race. In the United States white people tend to give way to black people regardless of whether they are on their own or in a group. In the United Kingdom, single black pedestrians tend to give way to single white pedestrians. However, group size takes precedence over race and larger groups displace smaller ones regardless of the race of the people in the groups.

Getting about Besides walking, public transport is the most common form of movement in most large cities. The number of people moving around the city in any one day is enormous.

In London, which boasts the oldest underground system in the world (established in 1863), the system moves 3.5 million people each weekday through its 272 stations. At one underground station alone, Victoria, which is also a railway terminus, underground and bus terminus, the transport system carries over 80 million passengers per year. A similar number of people use New York's underground which covers 230 miles through 465 stations. In London, buses also carry about 3 million people daily and there is also a vast train network. With so many people on the move and often concentrating their travel around certain times, the density of travel in public transport is considerable.

TOURISTS

After the first week of living in New York . . . I was on the subway bitching about the tourists, and yet I wasn't really a New Yorker. It was just kind of a way to put them . . . say, 'Oh, goddamn, can't they move faster? You don't know where you're going.' And I had a map myself.

CLIFTON – New York

COMMUTING IN CROWDS

People [are] rushing out of the train who are late for work or wherever they're going, coming off of the train and they're rushing out; and you have people that are late for work rushing into the train. I have to weave to the left and to the right, and get by those outcoming commuters and get on the train before those doors close.

GERALD – New York

The crowdedness of the city works two ways. It stops you from being lonely, if you're inclined to feel that way. But I have to say . . . the one thing I seem to be more aware of is body odours . . . 'specially when I came back in that heat wave in the summer and the tubes were unbearable [but] that didn't stop me wanting to be here. . . I could do without having my face squashed into somebody's armpit in the middle of this heat wave!

SAUNDRA – London

Walking is more relaxed and less constrained in shopping malls, although people still obey unspoken rules which oil the flow of movement.

Territory

Primary territory: our homes Animals mark out their personal territory by means of a variety of signals and scents which indicate they will defend it aggressively if necessary. When outside their own territory, domestic animals such as dogs engage in temporary marking but are less likely to defend this territory. Often when they meet some other dog in a more public terrain which has been marked by many other dogs, they move into a series of sniffing rituals to decide on a response.

The primary territory of humans is their home or land. Ownership is documented by means of a contract and other formal records, but is also usually signalled by physical boundaries such as fences and doors. The defence of this space is enshrined in law and anybody crossing the boundaries without permission faces potential sanctions. Underlying territorial possession is the idea of control. Owners are seen to have absolute control over their primary space. Clear markers of ownership such as signs and boundaries serve to prevent any invasion.

Animals exhibit less conflict when the ownership of space is clearly demarcated. There is some suggestion that a similar situation may prevail for humans. Where the ownership of primary areas is distinguished unambiguously, relationships may be more harmonious. However, the unambiguous marking of territory (and the resulting harmonious relationships) can only occur when those involved accept the boundaries. The possession of broader based territories can be seen with urban gangs who mark the boundaries of their territory with graffiti. The acceptance by other gangs of these boundaries reduces conflict, and gang conflict arises where territory is disputed, and when the boundaries are less clear or not marked.

Our cars The car in modern life is sometimes an interesting extension of primary territory. It is treated as a moveable space, much like the extension of a home which is decorated and personalized like the interior of a house to mark its owner. It is also defended with the additional backup of legal sanction.

We treat our cars as pets. We give them names, carefully groom them, and protect them when faced by threats from others. We even construct houses for them to live in next to us. For those without a garage, the importance of being able to park directly outside the home goes way beyond either comfort or necessity. It

CAR AS EXTENSION OF HOME

. . . I carry a lot of things in my car, a lot of my books, clothes, things that I might need through the day if I'm going out after work. So it would be very difficult and look quite embarrassing for me to carry around my pyjamas – because I stayed at my friend's house last night – and walk around with big bags all day. It wouldn't feel right for me. So my car's good for me in that sense as well.

PINKY – London

I live about one minute from an underground [station] and when I get home midday, early afternoon, it's impossible to park. All the commuters park in our street, so I have to circle round looking for a place to park, and I often can't park in my own street until about seven or eight o'clock at night.

ARTHUR – London

means we can keep an eye on our pet. In return, cars protect us from the outside world by offering us a home on wheels, at least for the time we are travelling. We personalize them to make them more our own and like many of our homes, collect all sorts of things in them.

The dilemma for many car owners is that the space is continually on the move. In older cities where there are no garages or carports to house cars, a dominant concern is where they are parked. Many car owners in the United Kingdom believe that according to some law of natural justice the area of the road immediately outside their house is for their car, in order to bring it closer to their immovable space, their house.

Driving anger The security the car offers us is an important feature of city life. We are able to travel at great speed through dark and unfriendly areas protected by our personal ring of steel. That refuge in turn can make us aggressive to others in ways we would not dream of being when out in the open. The ability of drivers to hurl abuse, flash signs and shout insults at

A recent survey showed that one in six drivers was subject to road rage.

one another from the cover of their car has become a daily experience. It is as if the car offers us anonymity. It not only shields us, but also offers the safeguard of a quick getaway. The possibility that we may be abusing a neighbour, friend or work colleague is something to which we barely give a thought. The recently coined 'road rage' gives us a term on which to hang extremes of this behaviour. A recent survey in the UK showed that one in every six drivers was subjected to road rage in the past year. In most cases they were forced to give way, but in 800,000 cases, people were physically threatened.

Research suggests there are seven different things which trigger driving anger: hostile gestures, illegal driving, driving that is too slow, a police presence, speeding in urban areas, discourtesy, and traffic obstructions. Although men and women are equally likely to become angry when driving, they respond to different triggers. Men are more angered by the presence of police and slow drivers, women by illegal behaviour and traffic obstructions. Studies suggest people with specific types of personality become angry when driving. Competitiveness is one feature which makes everyone more susceptible to anger on the road. People often speed up and close a gap when someone else wants to slip in to a line of traffic. The time saved in many attempts to beat other cars is often a few

ROAD RAGE AND THE CAR AS PROTECTIVE SHIELD

I really get mad. I'd really like to crash my car into everybody to teach them a lesson for being in my way. I get really mad. I start screaming in my car. I probably yell and call people names in my car much more than I would if I was just walking on the streets. I make gestures at them; sometimes they will make gestures back. I scream at them, call them names.

VERONICA – Los Angeles

I feel within my car it's my domain, and it's almost like a fortress. I'm protected . . . very seldom do you actually have to take responsibility for insulting someone, or honking, or expressing your anger in some other fashion, gestures and whatnot. So I think of it as being a pretty safe place. . . . People can get quite violent and I think if the consequences were less dire, people would crash in to each other to express their disgust, as if it were really bumper cars.

MARY – New York

I've been known to, like, scream in a car. I've let a driver next to me know how unhappy I am with a little digit display or something. It depends on where I'm at in the day; it can range from screaming to something a little less intense. But that's it; that's where I kind of lose it.

RICHARD – New York

. . . I will kill myself or kill somebody driving. . . . I sometimes get so furious with myself when I'm late to get somewhere. The things I've done to drivers in the past and the names that I've called them: I'm surprised that I'm still living and walking.

PINKY – London

If you get somebody who's doddling along at 20 miles [32km] an hour causing a tail-back, or somebody cuts you out or cuts in front of you, I get quite annoyed, shall we say. The old finger on the button, rude signs, bad language, the usual. I'd like to think that I had better self-control than that, but that's the way it goes. It's just the car seems to change a personality. You get behind the wheel and you become a different person sometimes. I don't know why it is, it just is.

ARTHUR – London

seconds, but is felt as a huge achievement in the competitive world of commuting.

Driving behaviour is in sharp contrast to our demeanour when walking. As walkers, it is unthinkable that we would cut in front of someone or refuse to give way or gesticulate rudely at them.

Other personal places in the city People tend to take possession of other areas in public arenas as their own territory, such as desks at school or college, a particular place in the library, or space around a desk in an open-plan office. Clear signals of ownership are made by personalizing these desks with a photograph, a name plate and sundry other articles indicating that the space is occupied and that use requires permission.

Some semi-public areas are not exactly personal territory but are shared by a group. Examples of this kind of space are private clubs, where the space is reserved for a group and will be defended by that group. Some bars, although notionally public, have become the ownership of a particular group. When an unwitting stranger walks into these situations they are given signals that the area is 'under ownership'. These may include frosty glances, silence, turning away etc.

Public space City dwellers have learnt to co-operate in a subtle set of rules about space in public places, because when people are in public places the territory is not marked for anyone in particular. Everyone has equal rights to it and territory can only be transiently possessed. The way this is achieved is governed by a series of conventions or rules used to mark possession of space.

A classic example is to place a coat over a chair while queuing for food in a busy restaurant. The use of a personal article as a sign to mark temporary possession of an area is an alternative to the scent sprayed by some animals. It is an appropriate signal for the objective because the same space will change ownership countless times during the course of a day.

These behaviours are governed by implicit rules and, therefore, require the agreement of others. They can be a point of conflict when the tacit agreement breaks down or is misinterpreted. Implicit rules can easily be broken and will be if someone moves the coat off the chair and occupies the table. The displaced person may restrict their behaviour to the non-verbal expressions of displeasure such as angry glances, huffing and puffing and grunts. A slightly raised level of territorial defence is when a person tells someone else they had marked/booked the place in the knowledge that the conversation can be overheard. On some occasions they may challenge outright the person or group who displaced them.

Marking territory in public space has been well studied in libraries. Here the use of territorial markers with open books, coats or a newspaper work effectively when density levels are low. With increased density, objects that are clearly personal, such as a coat, are more effective than impersonal markers like a library book.

The essence of territorial possession is that a person has control, for varying degrees of time, over an area of space. With a home, this may be years; for a table in a restaurant it may be for a very short period.

The regularity with which we occupy public space can create a familiarity with others who frequent that same space. Perhaps ironically, this may lead to the development of quite close relationships and in their own way, a sense of community that is particular to the urban milieu. These informal communities make a city less anonymous and create a sense of belonging.

The rules governing the rights of control over public spaces in cities, with the large numbers of people, is essential for the harmony of city life. The codes are unwritten and their limits often culturally defined, but carefully regulated through social interaction. Feedback when the codes are broken and intervention by others help to keep transgressors in place.

An extreme variant of this, and somewhat less harmonious, is the technique used by young urban groups and gangs to communicate ownership of space which reflects back to the animal-like behaviour of territorial marking. Studies of teenage gangs in the United States demonstrate how graffiti is a signal to other groups of ownership of an area, and simultaneously, an assertion of the identity and control of the group. It is literally seen as marking the edges of a space that has been claimed. What is interesting is that the marked space is often only considered invaded when it is crossed by a rival gang. Many inhabitants who are not of the specific age or reference group do not recognize or respond to the graffiti signals. The signals are rather like a special language between certain social groups.

GANG TERRITORIES

If you know where the boundary is you don't wear all red and you don't want to wear all blue. You want to stay as neutral as possible. Or if you want to wear them colours, wear something to break it off: I mean break the colours off. If you want to wear a top, wear a top with some blue jeans and some shoes or tennis shoes, just something casual. Over there is the . . . you know . . . you find out what they're wearing. You can see what they're wearing. That's how you find out your borderline, with what they're wearing.

DANIEL – Los Angeles

Privacy

Being alone Retaining a sense of privacy goes a long way to explain much of our behaviour in cities and crowded places. By preserving a sense of privacy we are able to maintain a sense of self identity. It is a way of promoting a sense of personal autonomy instead of always being enveloped in a group and conforming to group norms.

Private times are times when there is freedom from the expectations of the group. When we are on our own there are no requirements to fulfil social roles. For example, time away from work colleagues means freedom from being judged and the ability to relax and let down our guard. It also means time for reflection about our actions with others. We are able to remove our public persona when truly private and need no longer be concerned about being viewed and judged. This has been referred to as 'emotional release', as we no longer have to be careful in our behaviour and can express our emotions as we actually feel them because we are not under any social obligations.

One of the most important functions of privacy is to regulate the number of people with whom we have to interact. The large number of people with whom we come into contact living in a city means there is an enormous potential claim on our attention, our emotions, our time, our involvement from others. By seeking privacy and signalling it to others, we avoid this encumbrance. In the city we deliberately avoid many social contacts and limit the number of people with whom we interact. The behaviour that allows us to do this would undoubtedly and justifiably be considered rude and unfriendly were it to occur in a small town or a rural environment. In the city, it enables us to survive.

Eye contact and regulating interaction One way in which we try to regulate how many people we interact with in the city is in relation to eye contact. One of the functions of eye contact is to initiate a connection with somebody. But in many public settings, such as underground trains, buses, or walking on the street, city dwellers usually try to avoid initiating social contact. Meeting someone's gaze in a public environment where it is more typical to avoid interactions is likely to be considered inappropriate behaviour for that setting. Being caught looking at someone causes embarrassment to many people as it breaks the code of that environment. In situations perceived to be potentially threatening, people react to a gaze by standing farther back and using personal space as a buffer zone.

It is common in cities to avoid social contact by wearing sunglasses. This makes it difficult for others to have eye contact with you and hence, initiate a social interaction. Another tactic is the development of the middle distance stare. By staring into the middle distance with no particular focus, especially when others are in close proximity, such as in lifts or on public transport, we don't allow eye contact. These are both effective ways of reducing the number of approaches by strangers.

We sometimes use eye gaze to prevent social interaction. Typically, a stare in a public situation may be responded to by a challenge such as returning the stare. This may be designed simply to embarrass the other person or it may be aggressive, going so far as a verbal challenge. These techniques are designed to halt the intrusion of others.

One of the reasons why residential crowding is so difficult to cope with, and has a larger effect on psychological well-being than public crowding, is that the most common area where privacy is obtained is at home. In a crowded residence it is much more difficult to find a place for privacy or to avoid unwanted social interactions.

Being private In many situations a person's privacy is invaded and he or she has to indicate the need to return to a private time. This can be especially difficult in public situations such as bumping into friends or acquaintances, for example in a restaurant or on a train journey. In some situations, the way to return to privacy is to be direct and state the desire to have privacy. Many people find the directness difficult, first because there is a general expectation that to be alone is not desirable, and second, because directness is often interpreted as rudeness. Consciously or not, however, our non-verbal behaviour often gives off signals that we do not want company. Avoiding of eye contact or beginning to fidget are common signals that we use and receive from others.

People have become particularly adept at finding private places in the city.

Being crowded in a subway car – sometimes it's kind of an interesting exercise in self-containment, in discipline, because everyone else is going through the same process too. I think there's a lot of empathy, and that's a situation where you will find that people just kind of ease off. Nobody wants to bother anyone or make eye contact; they just turn into their own capsule.

JOHN – New York

My stairwell has six flights of stairs. People walk past and you just don't make eye contact. Everyone looks down or looks up or looks to the side.

CLIFTON – New York

Eye contact can initiate or regulate social contact; staring into the middle distance in a confined space like a lift is an effective way of preventing interaction.

We steal private time and space opportunistically in situations when we are doing something else. Time alone in the elevator allows us to adjust our clothes or hair. Going to the toilet serves both its traditional function as well as time alone behind a closed door to reflect and take a breather.

Interestingly, the presence of certain people does not constitute an invasion of privacy. Notable amongst these are taxi drivers and waiters. People are normally quite content to continue intimate conversations and conduct in the face of these particular people who play the role of the 'inattentive observer'. Their behaviour supports this notion, as they adopt an air of not concentrating on the action that is being played out in front of them. The players are happy to accept this guise, often knowing full well that they are being closely observed.

Besides using various places, we also attempt to obtain privacy by using other techniques to restrict the entry of others into our world. None has been as dramatic as the developing use of the personal stereo. The use of a personal stereo restricts other people's access to us because they will judge that they are interrupting an activity. It also enables the listener to withdraw with a 'middle distance stare', avoiding making eye contact with others and thereby initiating an interaction.

Being fooled by privacy: the car The car's special place in the city extends into the world of privacy. Our sense of privacy and comfort in the car leads us to believe we are insulated from the outside world and no longer on the stage. We therefore feel able to conduct a whole range of personal activities in the car in full view of others.

When inside their cars, people feel they are in a private, invisible world.

Personal space

Psychological space Besides attempts to retain privacy which are efforts to withdraw physically or psychologically from the social world into a private world, city dwellers have had to adapt and make changes to their personal space. Personal space is a psychological construct referring to the physical distance or boundary we all attempt to maintain between ourselves and the people around us. In general, this space is roughly circular but with a larger space in front than behind. We find ourselves being comfortable with a particular distance between ourselves and others around us and will move to regulate this distance. The exact distance is dependent upon a number of individual, social and particularly in the city, situational factors. In the city we find it hard to keep people out of our space bubbles and to escape.

Personal space has a number of different definitions depending on the distances we feel comfortable with for different situations. At the individual level, we generally reserve what is referred to as 'intimate distance' for close intimate relationships. Research finds this to be between 0 to 45cm (18in). It often involves physical contact and when looking at someone, visual distortion the closer we get. This distance is too close for acquaintances, and people can be seen withdrawing in certain social situations when the distance between them narrows to this amount.

Personal space refers to the physical distance we are comfortable with between ourselves and people around us. Other animals are less constrained.

The distance we generally use for conversing with family and friends (close distances) and business colleagues (further distances) is called 'personal distance' and has been found to be between 45cm and 1.2m (1½ and 4ft). We use a moderate level of voice, and unlike in intimate relationships, at the further levels of personal distance the only odours detectable are those deliberately displayed such as perfumes and after-shave lotions.

'Social distance' may be seen at times of impersonal transactions, such as purchasing something in a shop. It involves more formal contacts where status and decorum are retained. It can occur at a close range, found to be between 1.2 and 2.14m (4 and 7ft) or at a far range, between 2.14 and 3.65m (7 and 12ft).

'Public distance' is used where a speaker addresses an audience and could be between 3.65 and 7.6m (12 and 25ft) in some situations and further than 7.6m (25ft) in others.

Getting too close There are a number of theories about the role played by personal space. One suggests that the regulation of distance from others is a way of protecting ourselves from threat. We only let people we know well approach close to us, and we keep strangers at a distance which makes us less vulnerable to attack. Personal space also allows us to indicate the kind of relationship we wish to have with someone. Intimate relationships are signalled by close proximity, and when that intimacy is refused, individuals withdraw to signal their refusal. The closeness of individuals, although subject to gender differences in many cultures, tends to reflect the degree of attraction between individuals.

Children do not appear to have the same personal space as adults which suggests that it is learned behaviour. The size of personal space gradually increases from the age of three, up to twenty-one years of age. Other evidence suggesting that personal space is learned comes from the small but observable differences in personal space by different cultures and subcultures.

The shape of personal space can be altered by where we are looking. If we

---

TOUCHING

It's not so bad if you're not touching, but once the bodies start touching it's very uncomfortable. I mean, I don't mind the crowds, but if my hand has to be next to another person's hand, or you can't move your body, you can start feeling claustrophobic. I'm not scared in those types of situations, but I don't like having to touch other people.

LEANNE – New York

I think being in New York is actually helping me deal with this, because before, if somebody would sit next to me, I would be like, 'Oh, you're going to have to move over, that's all there is to it.' And here you actually have to sit near people that are touching you on the subway, and that's really strange.

SHERRIE – New York

The distance we maintain between ourselves and others varies according to whether they are friends or strangers.

turn our head to one side then the distance of personal space extending forward is significantly reduced. When we turn our head forward then the length of personal space extending forward is returned to its original value.

Touch and taboo Touch is the most intimate of social contacts and is the primary system for expressing and experiencing affection, inclusion, and control. In particular, it is used as a signal of intimacy. As such, it is the most carefully regulated and guarded aspect of our communications with one another, and is subject to the most taboos.

The rules of touch in relation to gender are clearly defined in different cultures and subcultures. For example, in the United States, hand holding was found to be acceptable and expected, but face touching and an arm around the waist or shoulder were seen as violations of expectations of behaviour in public.

When strangers meet, although it may invade personal space, the function of touch has an interesting effect. In studies where individuals were asked to help a stranger with a task, where the stranger touched the individual they tended to be more likely to assist. It is as if the touch signals an intimacy or a power in the relationship encouraging an obligation to assist.

Involuntary touch between strangers in the city is inevitable and most city dwellers have become adapted to it. But it is disliked and often an involuntary touch, especially if it is skin to skin, such as when you overhand someone else's hand on the strap of a subway train. This customarily leads to an apology; it still carries with it the taboo.

Invading space When our personal space is invaded we tend to become aroused. If it is invaded by someone to whom we are attracted the arousal is certainly experienced as pleasurable. In contrast, we tend to feel uncomfortable when our personal space is invaded by strangers. Although there are individual differences to the space, the closer a stranger comes the more aroused we become. The degree of discomfort that we feel is directly related to the amount of distance invaded.

When space is invaded by strangers one of the most common responses is to move away from the situation. Some interesting studies have been done in libraries. Someone allied to the investigator would pull up a chair and sit at a specified distance from the subject of study. At close distances some individuals would withdraw and on occasions leave the library. Others initiated a series of non-verbal behaviour to build up

Although these benches are designed for two people, we will generally not sit next to someone if there is an alternative seat available.

It's awkward when you're literally crushed into a small tube [on the underground] and you want to make that journey. You don't want to wait for the next tube and you apologize as you get on, but still push right inside, right up to some-body and just squash them completely. Bend your head into their head as the doors close and completely crush them. You breathe in. You make sure you don't sneeze and you try to avoid complete eye contact. Even though your eye is right next to somebody else's, you'll look wherever you can to avoid them. The trouble is that there's six other eyes right in front of you.

ALEX – London

If I'm in a crowd and I'm kinda stuck in the middle of people, I really get freaked out. It's almost like a claustro-phobic feeling. I've got to have some elbow space. I've got to have this kind of secret protection around me. It's almost like a protective shield, where people can't get to me . . . So when people start getting a little too close I break out the elbows and give them a good stiff . . . It's like this is my space and this is your space, and it's OK if you're in your space, but the minute you come into my space it's not OK.

KENYA – Los Angeles

barriers between themselves and the person invading their personal space. These typically consisted of facing away from the invader, pulling in their shoulders, and putting up objects between them-selves and the invader.

The city and personal space

In the city there are countless situations where the general rules of personal space are overwhelmed. Any trip in a crowded underground train or standing in a bus involves close physical contact with strangers, as we have already seen. Simply walk-ing through shopping crowds involves physical contact with strangers.

The city has created a different culture of personal space by defin-ing many situations as ones where personal space will be invaded and the option of flight is removed. Consequently, city dwellers have developed finely honed skills to deal with situations where proximity is so close as to be at the intimate level with strangers. It is quite acceptable to be in physical contact with strangers in these situations but we still use classic strategies of non-verbal signals to create barriers between ourselves and others. We withdraw our bodies, turn away from people in crowded situations, try to avoid skin-to-skin contact and apologize when our hands touch. Turning away is a technique that we know reduces the extent of our personal space in a forward direction. City people have become skilled at interposing a newspaper or book between themselves and others around them.

We also avoid eye contact as this is the signal to initiate a conversation. Instead, in the absence of a book or newspaper, we adopt the middle dis-tance stare, an unfocused steady look across the crowd or in elevators at the indicator as the lift moves.

Often when commuting we use our newspaper as a barrier, but the barrier itself can be used to invade our space. When someone attempts to read our newspaper on the train or bus we often behave as if the newspaper were part of our territory and make defensive moves.

In situations where we are moving and are likely to break the taboo of physical contact by brushing up against someone, we need to signal the meaning of the touch. The quick apology when passing is well developed in the city, and is commonly used when in a hurry.

Watching others   Gaze is the one technique that can bridge distance. When someone looks across space and stares or looks frequently at someone else it is often interpreted as a desire to initiate a relationship. Alternatively, the stare can be used as a threat. Whatever the purpose, the unwanted gaze from someone in a crowded situation, is perceived as an invasion of personal space, even though it does not involve touch or close physical contact.

The response to this is likely to be the same as the response to any invasion of personal space. If the gaze or invasion persists, then the response sometimes becomes hostile rather than defensive. The stare is so effective at bridging social distance that it can even invade the boundary established by the car. Motorists have been found to pull off faster from a traffic light when they have been subjected to a stare from a pedestrian or a motorcycle rider.

The difficulty for city dwellers is that they are frequently engaged in people-watching which for many, is the dominant sport of *homo urbanus*. Frequently people-watching has to be surreptitious and the return gaze is an indication that we have been found out. Many cities are designed to facilitate people-watching. The design of pavement cafes enables individuals to watch passers-by. In some situations it is appropriate and admissible to stare at others. Certain areas of many cities are designed for parading. In places such as this people dress up in order to be looked at. In some cases people-watching is done from a distance and needs special equipment.

City life is not a constant battle for space and privacy. Humans are a social species and generally choose to go where others are. This allows us to look at other people, but we tread a fine line between people watching and intrusive staring.

READING SOMEONE'S PAPER IN A CROWD

I feel a little embarrassed because they caught me, and I know that I'm not supposed to be doing that. Sometimes I can tell they know that I'm reading so they may open it a little wider, but most people don't like people to read over their shoulder, so usually they'll turn away or flip the pages really fast, so I stop.

LEANNE – New York

*Looking over some-
one's shoulder to
read their magazine
can feel invasive.*

I stare at a lot of people's books, reading material, and I get very defensive, I find, when people do that to me. When people are looking at my magazine, at my newspaper, I react the same way. I guard it or like, look: 'What's your problem?' kind of thing. 'Are you looking at me?'

JOHN – New York

It can be made worse by somebody reading your paper on the tube. Once or twice I've actually given the newspaper to some-body because they're having a good read. They're enjoying it more than I am. It embarrasses them very much because it's done in front of others.

KHALID – London

SOMEONE READING YOUR PAPER IN A CROWD

I'm guilty of the same thing. They might just have like a really interesting magazine or something, which I can understand, but if I am not in the mood for somebody to be looking over my shoulder, and I move away, and they keep doing it. Most normal people won't do that. The only person who's going to do that is somebody who's like a little off or something, or they must really be interested in the story. I don't really like people looking over my shoulder.

LEANNE - New York

*Staring pointedly at someone is
a way of repulsing unwanted
attention.*

When I look at other people's magazines or newspapers, when I peer over and look I find that they feel, like almost naked. They sort of hide or guard their reading material from me. I feel like a sort of a pervert actually, almost like a peeping Tom. I don't have much experience in that area, but I assume that's what a peeping Tom would feel like. People just basically give me dirty looks. They sort of carry it with them, with their body manner-isms, like they're guarding it.

JOHN - New York

find: all children\good

One of the dominant sports for homo urbanus is people watching

Chapter 3

Interacting

. . . then we sit and sob and long for the gas-lit streets and sound of human voices. Let us gather together in the great cities, and light huge bonfires of a million gas jets, and shout and sing together and feel brave.
JEROME K JEROME, *Three Men in a Boat*

Mixing in the city

In the modern city we are used to moving through an ocean of strangers with ease. But this is very different from the experience of our ancestors. In traditional society, the place where someone lived largely determined the people with whom they interacted. Limited forms of transport and an economy tied to the soil meant that people often lived and worked in the same place. Therefore, there was a high degree of relatively personal communication with others in the immediate locality. Most people in that locality would have been familiar with each other, not only as individuals, but as family groups. They also would have been known by their occupation in relation to the local economy of that community.

By contrast, in the city, friendships span wider geographical areas and are based more on shared interests than shared neighbourhoods. Nonetheless, in cities the possibilities of chance meetings with friends and acquaintances occur more than would be predicted by statistical probability. This is because people who are friends share similar interests, behaviours, and values, and are more likely to frequent similar places in the city. The notion of a 'neighbourhood' or 'community' in a metropolis needs to be conceived of in relation to a wider range of activities than those that take place just where people reside.

Moving through an ocean of strangers is an everyday experience for city dwellers.

A sense of place

Neighbourhoods There is a commonly held view that cities are no more than a series of neighbourhoods, each with its own distinctive character whose inhabitants tend to mix together and have a sense of belonging to their area. Some social commentators suggest this is now in decline, but such a view is questionable.

To a degree London, like many other cities, retains a sense of local community where individuals feel they are part of a particular neighbourhood and obtain some of their identity from it. Despite the changes many cities are going through, there does seem to remain a sense of community for many residents. Studies show people's feelings of grief at being relocated from one neighbourhood to another. Residents often exhibit strong expressions of identity with certain areas, even when they are deprived and run-down. People also often refuse to move from a locality even when it has been subject to a natural disaster.

The type of neighbourhood is extremely important. When people move from one city to another they attempt to replicate the type of neighbourhood in which they lived before. So, people who previously lived in the inner city try to do likewise in their new city. When people cannot find a similar environment to the one they had before, a lot of energy and resources are put into reproducing it.

This is particularly obvious in the case of migrants who try to recreate the physical and social characteristics of the country of their birth. The result is that a series of ethnic neighbourhoods are produced. The presence of large numbers of immigrants contributes to the sense of change and dynamism that characterizes so many cities.

So, even when they move regularly, people take with them a sense of place by moving to, or recreating, similar types of neighbourhoods to the ones they have left.

In general, the size, density and mobility of the urban population has not led to a breakdown in the sense of community. It has been augmented by a variant form of community. Regular face-to-face chance meetings in the local neighbourhood leading to associations and groupings, have been gradually replaced with associations between people based upon areas of shared interest. Increasing opportunities to network and communicate far afield, as well as greater mobility, means city dwellers are able to establish alliances based not only on proximity, but on shared interests. So, those with a particular interest congregate regardless of where they live.

NEIGHBOURHOODS

I've made a village of my experiences in London. I've chosen my friends and I've got my neighbours around me and that's my little kind of village.

ALEX – London

*Individuals often feel a
close sense of identity
with their neighbour-
hoods.*

City neighbourhoods have thus evolved from providing the primary and
unique community group for many individuals, to being places with which
they have a limited form of identification. The neighbourhood for many city
dwellers is now principally the place in which they live and from where
they travel to work and other interests.

   The idea that the 'geographic neighbourhood community' has been
replaced by the 'spatially dispersed interest community', leading to a
completely different organization of cities, however, is an overstatement.
Geographically defined neighbourhoods have not been transformed into
anonymous places, and for many people, the area they live in still retains a
degree of neighbourhood feel. Interestingly, the characteristics which
contribute towards this sense of community seem to be similar to those
normally associated with small town and rural environments. Just as
inter-country migrants preserve aspects of their previous life that were
functional for them, so too might city dwellers be combining aspects of a
more traditional life with the newer advantages of city living. *Homo urbanus*
seems to want to both have his cake and eat it!

A number of factors influence this feeling of belonging to, and identifying with, the area in which you live. One is known as 'behavioural rootedness'. Those people who are well established in their community tend to identify a sense of community. For example the longer someone lives in an area the greater is their sense of community. In the United States, people who own their properties also express more of a sense of community or neighbourhood than those who do not.

The second general factor which encourages a sense of community is known as 'social bonding'. Individuals who can identify more of their neighbours by first names are found to be more connected to their local area and feel a greater sense of neighbourhood. More detailed studies show a third factor which is important in identifying a sense of community to be a sense of 'social cohesiveness'. A high sense of social cohesiveness tends to occur when neighbours see a lot of each other, have feelings of mutual involvement, a tendency to gossip together, and a strong disapproval of deviancy.

BELONGING TO A NEIGHBOURHOOD

Well, you don't want to get lost in the wrong neighbourhood if you don't belong there. Not that there is anything wrong with that neighbourhood, but it's kind of an unspoken thing that people have their neighbourhoods, and you really aren't welcome there, for whatever reason. I think it's wise to choose where you're welcome and where you're not, and you don't want to invade people's space.

SCOTT – Los Angeles

I wouldn't go through Beverly Hills at night – some place like real quiet and residential – because they will lift their noses at me. I feel real uneasy going through a place like Beverly Hills. I wouldn't go where I feel uncomfortable; very, very uncomfortable.

DANIEL – Los Angeles

In New York, a neighbourhood identifies itself to you as being treacherous. You pick up on the clues. Some of it's the music that's being played around you; it's whether or not the streets are clean; it's who's hanging out on the stoop.

RICHARD – New York

City people Research suggests that city dwellers develop an identification with a general type of neighbourhood, not just a specific area. Although New Yorkers may identify themselves specifically with New York, and Londoners with London, they also tend to have an overriding sense of identity which embraces a particular kind of environment – the metropolitan. They recognize something integral to themselves that is linked to a city neighbourhood and would usually rather locate to another city with all that it has to offer, than a rural or out-of-city environment. Their own identity is caught up with the characteristics of the environment. When we move from one urban environment to another, we take with us general categories of what urban life consists of, which have been partly learned from our previous city experiences. We have city stereotypes in our heads and use these notions or cognitions to interpret and judge the qualities of our new city of residence. It is this generalized conception of place that city dwellers use to identify with a type of locale.

People

Seas of strangers In downtown New York there are about a quarter of a million people within a ten-minute walking radius. Add to this the fact that because of technology we are free of the geographic constraints of the neighbourhood, the city offers the possibility of countless potential relationships. What is interesting is that we restrict the numbers of people we see and know. It is as if there is a psychological limitation on the number or people we can or maybe want to deal with and who are, as a result, available to us for social interaction. These are not the people we can rely on as close friends but the people whom we know sufficiently well in our worlds with whom we could potentially have a social interaction. This number has been found to vary between 600 (Mexico City), 2,025 (Orange County, California) and 1,700 (Florida).

However, like the physical stimuli of the city, there are too many people for *homo urbanus* to attend to. We suffer from people overload in the city. There are a number of ways in which we cope with the pressure of all the people around us. One is to speed up and so limit our contacts. For example, when we bump into an acquaintance in the street, we are careful to give ourselves the option of slipping away quickly. Our body language and style of conversation indicates that time is pressing and we must soon be moving on.

We treat certain types of communication as formal – when no attempt is made to befriend the individual. When we buy our newspaper in the morning, we restrict our interaction to the purely functional exchange. It is a form of interaction which does not allow any bonds to develop.

In certain situations intimate conversations are conducted despite the fact that they can obviously be over-heard. Many social interactions in the city remain functional, formal and fairly anonymous.

By keeping certain social exchanges to a minimum, we are able to reduce the amount of incoming information and not be overwhelmed. Thus, we retain some anonymity and this enables us to move through the city with a degree of speed and ease.

City dwellers tend not to start significant friendships or relationships with all the people with whom they potentially could do so. There are simply too many. Looking at the nature of our relationships with other people in the city we can see there are many types, which vary according to how close they are, namely

Immediate relatives and most intimate friends
Very close friends and other relations who we actively see
Close friends and relatives with whom we have passive relations
People with whom we have dealings and who do things for us
Acquaintances
People we recognize but don't always remember

Family ties still appear to play an important part of most relationships, regardless of the degree of urbanization. In particular, people often turn to families in times of crisis. Attaching numbers to the different types of relationships we have is difficult, as there is a large amount of individual variation. Some people are 'social lions' who value and cultivate friendships and alliances. At the other end of the spectrum are 'social recluses' who have low levels of interaction with others. Nonetheless, some estimates suggest that on average, people in the city have roughly 1,800 people whom they know and could potentially establish a social interaction. Out of these, they have active relationships with about twenty (1 per cent) and intimate relationships with about five.

Ritual relationships The city is full of relationships where the interaction consists of a ritual exchange. In many cases, these are where two people are involved in an exchange of goods and services. Purchasing a newspaper every morning from the paper seller involves a ritual exchange where some interaction takes place. To have the relationship develop into something more than an exchange of a greeting, the request

City dwellers do not normally engage in conversation with fellow commuters even though they may see them every day.

and perhaps a comment about the weather, is more than either party desires. We try to keep these ritualized relationships pleasant and brief. In the city there are too many other people with whom we interact and we need to limit how involved we get with others. Keeping a relationship to a ritualized exchange makes it predictable and controllable.

Similar behaviour prevails in relation to casual relationships. We have a large number of relationships with other people around us that we don't call friends, nor have more than a passing relationship with. For example, the commuter who stands on the platform to catch the same train every morning is often able to recognize others who catch it. This familiarity makes us feel comfortable but it is unlikely that we will strike up a conversation with these recognizable people. We wish to keep the relationship at this level.

This rule of behaviour may change if we see these people in a different context or environment. For example, if catching a plane to go on holiday, or going to a gym after work we recognize a fellow commuter, then the familiar face from the platform may be approached. It is as if we establish the relationship at a particular level by the place it occurs. When the place changes, then so too does our behaviour. The familiarity or recognition of a shared interest allows us to develop a different kind of relationship.

Is the city lonely? The difficulty with making friends in the city is often quoted as self evident and an example of the relative loneliness of many city dwellers. However, studies comparing the numbers of friends people have in urban and rural environments fail to find any significant differences. Although the evidence suggests that making friends is more difficult for newcomers, when people do move to the city, within seven or eight months they are usually able to build up a number of friendships equivalent to other city dwellers. The reason for their initial difficulty may be the suspicion and distrust that newcomers have for others in the city. It may also have something to do with the strategies (discussed earlier) that established city dwellers adopt for coping with the large numbers of people around them.

Being with other people Being in a group allows individuals to behave in certain ways, one of which is known as social facilitation. This is where the group makes it possible for the individual to act in certain ways. One particular aspect of social facilitation that has been studied is the time people spend in certain situations when they are on their own, compared with when they are in groups. Classic amongst these were early studies on how much time people spent drinking beer in bars. These studies showed that people on their own spent the shortest time in the bar and drank the least beer there, while those in groups spent longer times and as a result drank more. Those individuals who started off singly but were joined by others spent the longest time in the bar and as a result drank the most beer in the bar. Similar findings have been shown in other places where city dwellers congregate, such as coffee shops.

When individuals enter a densely packed social environment on their own, such as a coffee shop, they usually eat or read as well as drinking coffee. They often need to indicate to any observers that they have a purpose in going into a social environment other than social interaction with others. This is important, as when we are in social environments we know we are on a stage, and often want to give off signals to others that we are not lonely or in need of company as we have a task that we are involved in.

Making friends One of the pleasures of city life is that it no longer forces people to form relationships simply because they find themselves living or working near each other. The huge urban populations provide a critical mass of people and places where one can expect to find others who reflect our tastes.

Although some neighbourhoods still have an ethos of neighbourliness, cities' characteristics of increasing mobility, communications and diversity have made proximity much less important in determining friendship and feelings of affinity. To some degree, however, where we live still has an influence on who we meet and with whom we become friends.

Johnson studied the factors associated with friendship in an American city and found that having similar values and being seen as friendly, pleasant, polite, and easy to talk to were strong predictors of friendship. In contrast, how close people lived together (residential proximity) and worked together played a relatively modest role in stimulating friendship. Further confirmation of the breakdown of geographic locality in the city is provided by evidence from Toronto where researchers found three-quarters of people's active ties extended beyond the local city.

These findings are important as they illustrate the variety and choice of friendships that are available to city dwellers. Given the number of people with whom we come into contact, and the variety of places the city offers us to meet people with shared values, it is not surprising that proximity is no longer such an important factor in fostering friendship.

Neighbours

In general, city people no longer get their sense of identity from their neighbourhood, nor see it as the primary location for meeting people. Nonetheless, neighbours do still play an important role in some parts of their lives and neighbourliness can certainly affect the quality of home life.

Neighbourliness is the extent to which people living near each other engage informally, talk and visit, borrow and lend things. It also implies some degree of social support when it is needed and includes helping in emergencies. People tend to engage in these kinds of activities when they have a greater sense of community or neighbourliness, and in doing so, they also perpetuate and continue that ethos.

What do we want from neighbours?

Although generalizations are always difficult, the ideal city neighbour is often characterized as one who is there at times of need, such as watching over property, watering plants and receiving parcels on behalf of next-door neighbours who are out, but who places no major obligations other than reciprocal help, and creates no interference.

Neighbours are to be seen reassuringly in public areas but are not people with whom we necessarily wish to have an intimate relationship. Keeping the level of relationship with neighbours at this level involves not seeking help too frequently, and only rarely being in one another's homes. Managing neighbourly relationships is important because we endeavour to keep them at a friendly supportive level rather than allowing them to develop into fully blown friendships.

City talk

Face-to-face Face-to-face interactions involve both verbal and non-verbal exchanges. These are rich in content and we use both to convey a lot of information about our attitudes and feelings. It is the speed of verbal behaviour and exchange that characterizes city talk. Verbal exchanges in the city, particularly with strangers and in ritual relationships, are also noted for their brevity and may explain why people in the city are seen as unfriendly to many of those from the country.

Non-verbal interaction We very often reveal ourselves or impart information about how we are feeling through non-verbal behaviour, and we pick up non-verbal signals from other people. The non-verbal cues or signs we use to draw conclusions about other people, their character, intentions, feelings, views, thoughts, and so on, include facial expressions, body orientations, distance, touch, movements, and aspects of voice such as intonation and volume. Appearance and dress are also part of the non-verbal cues related to self-presentation.

Non-verbal behaviour is considered to be a spontaneous expression of an internal state of mind. As such, many scientists think non-verbal behaviour offers a true reflection of someone's internal feelings and expressions that are difficult to control. Others, in contrast, argue that we can control our presentation of self in the social world to some degree.

Some more obvious aspects of non-verbal behaviour, such as dress, are largely under voluntary control, but the interesting question is whether we can voluntarily control the disclosure of our internal emotions. The evidence suggests that many of our non-verbal facial expressions of emotion are not easily brought under voluntary control and likewise are difficult to produce on demand. Other non-verbal behaviours such as posture and movement are more easily voluntarily produced. One factor which influences the likelihood of emotions being expressed is how engrossed the individual is in the task they are doing. In many city behaviours, especially traversing a public area we are often not engrossed in what we are doing and able to control how we look to others. Indeed we may wish to portray a particular image as we move around public places.

Nonetheless, on the stage of the city, we do try and bring our non-verbal behaviours under control. We try to present ourselves to others in ways that will allow us to claim identities and persona we find desirable, think others will like, and sense are believable. The ways in which we use non-verbal behaviour to facilitate this presentation is something that is learned, and as a result, differs in different groups.

However, presenting ourselves in a particular way is not always easy,

Non-verbal signs such as our posture, facial expressions, hesitant body movements indicate a lot about our feelings.

and we don't have absolute control to present ourselves in any way we like. For example, some men may wish to appear cool and relaxed in many busy or threatening situations. Their emotions of fear may leak through their attempts at controlling their presentation. The situation may reduce the ability of the person to present in a particular way. Another set of circumstances may help a self-presentation. For example, a normally inhibited individual may feel able to let themselves go at a rock concert and present as an extrovert, because others are engaging in the same behaviour. The crowd acts as a facilitator for the self-presentation such a person might ordinarily find difficult.

The way in which emotions are expressed is directly related to the group or subculture to which we belong. Being cool and abstracted from the rush and noise of the city is a presentation which many city dwellers have developed. It is almost a technique to cut off their expressiveness. More importantly, it controls the exposure of the self to the world.

Signalling relationships

Non-verbal behaviour can be used to signal to people such as casual observers, the nature of our relationship with others. Couples walking along hand in hand in the city express to others the nature of their relationship. Similarly, wearing the traditional engagement or wedding ring indicates our affiliation with somebody who may be absent. This kind of behaviour is seen in a range of societies. It also, of course, offers a mechanism for rebellion and thus putting across more subtle messages such as not wearing a wedding ring when married.

When we are interacting in a public place, we need to and sometimes cannot help the expression of emotion. This is particularly helpful in busy streets where the ambient noise level is often high. In general, these expressions are considered to be important adjuncts to our self expression. Because noise levels are high we may exaggerate our non-verbal expressions so as to accurately convey what we are feeling.

Blushing and embarrassment   Blushing is a uniquely human attribute. It occurs when small blood vessels in the blush region (face, neck and ears) dilate causing increased blood flow with resulting flushing. Many people know they are blushing because they feel a warmth, but this does not always occur. Blushing is a good example of non-verbal behaviour which appears to be beyond our control. Blushing is often accompanied by averting the gaze, a self-conscious smile, and dysfluency in speech and movement.

Blushing has been discussed for many years. Darwin first wrote about it in 1872. It appears to occur in situations when we are discomforted, for instance, when we behave out of character, do something we know we shouldn't such as telling a lie, or perform incompetently. This led many to believe that blushing was an extension of embarrassment. But blushing also occurs in other situations. It can happen when we are placed under scrutiny such as in an interview, or are made the centre of attention in a group such as being praised at a dinner party, or even when we are simply being looked at by others.

Receiving unwanted attention is something that occurs with frequency in the city because we are constantly interacting with others. On many occasions, the exchanges are kept at an impersonal level, such as buying a ticket for the movies or collecting dry cleaning. When the status of the exchange changes because someone is subjected to increased scrutiny then we may blush. We spend a lot of time in the city watching other people. If seen doing so, we may blush at having broken the norms of behaviour. At

It is easy to identify the nature of some relationships by observing non-verbal behaviour, as with this couple happily embracing without reference to anyone around them.

the same time, others might also blush when subject to this social scrutiny.

On the public stage of the street we are often aware of being observed. Thus, we frequently feel constrained to offer some form of explanation, directed to nobody in particular, when we make a mistake in public. Classic amongst these is when we find ourselves going in the wrong direction. To signal to other people that we are not crazy we may offer an explanation, perhaps a look at the watch, or a mutter about having to go somewhere else. These kinds of behaviour are ways in which we regulate the observance of our public selves in the close confines of the city.

Telephone talk The telephone has become the tool by which city dwellers maintain contact with their friends and relatives in the city's dispersed villages. Although the phone allows us to stay in touch, it has also enabled us to live further apart. In the modern city our neighbourhoods are no longer physical: they are psychological. And the phone has not only changed the means by which we communicate, it has also changed the way in which we communicate by depriving us of the visual cues we rely on in face-to-face contact.

In fact, the growth of the telephone culture has led to the development of a different form of communication between people. In most industrialized countries there is at least one telephone for every household. Many have more than one telephone. Even in the cities of many developing countries phones within households have proliferated. In Beijing, some 63 per cent of all households now have a telephone.

I was sitting there watching the performance and all of a sudden my mobile phone went off and I nearly died. So I grabbed it, and everybody could hear it. It's so embarrassing. I pulled it out and I turned it on to turn it off and I could hear this 'Aimee, Aimee, answer the phone.' Oh my God. I just had to unplug the battery. It was so mortifying.

AIMEE – London

I had one really embarrassing moment where I was coming up the steps out of the subway and my full weight in one leg came down on this guy's ankle. I'd been really concerned about my weight of recent; I'd put on a lot of weight. Generally in a situation like that, if you bump in to somebody, have somebody knock in to somebody, they say, 'Oh, don't worry about it.' This guy starting ringing out in pain: 'Oh, you arsehole, you stepped on my leg, you hurt me!'
The next thing I know the whole subway platform was staring at me. The fat guy who came down on this guy's leg. It was a real horrible situation. So I tried to help him, and he was like, 'Get your hands off of me, I think you've broken my ankle, you arsehole, get away from me!' And then you could hear everybody sort of chatting and mumbling: 'He did it, he did it, that guy stepped on that guy's leg.'
It was really really embarrassing. There was about fifty people; it was a rush hour kind of scene.

JOHN – New York

I was running for a train, like a lot of us do when you live in the city, and I had on a nice suit, nice tweed. This was Fifty-ninth Street in the heat of rush hour. So I'm running down the stairs and I see my door, and I just feel a little confident. I'm just about to get in there, when all of a sudden the bottom of my shoe, just slipped up on me; all of a sudden it was like I was on a piece of ice. I just slid in like I'm a first – going in to first base – trying to slide home, playing baseball. I tear up my suit. man, and all of a sudden I see all of these people looking around at me. That's one of my most embarrassing moments.

PEPSI – New York

Certain public spaces in the city can be taken over for private functions without embarassment.

The telephone is a crucial means of contact when the demands of city life make it difficult to see family and friends.

I use the phone a lot. There are a lot of people in my life, my family and stuff, that I only have a relationship with over the phone, like my sister. I just had a two-hour conversation the other day, and I find out everything that's going on in her life and my life, and we haven't seen each other in like a couple of years. But it's almost like a therapy thing.

SCOTT – Los Angeles

I'm always in touch. I call home three or four times a day. I've got my mobile phone with a message answering machine on the phone, and as well people can reach me by fax. They can fax me at the charity and then she'll call me up with messages. So I've got two unpaid secretaries, so to speak. It keeps me going.

SAUNDRA – London

The phone is my relationship. Because you have so much to do in your life, if you can do half of it on the phone you don't have to drive, you don't have to deal with the clerk or the teller or the checker, or whatever it is that you're doing. Also, the phone becomes your lifeline, basically, to your friends and family, because in your day-to-day life you're working one pocket of the town and they're an hour and forty-five minutes away. It's not feasible to go and see them every day and continue personal relationships.

ERROL – Los Angeles

The telephone is very important. You can't survive without it. I can't keep in contact. I don't think my friendships would last without it. I live on the upper West Side. I don't have friends in downtown or midtown; they all live on the upper West Side. One on the upper East and that's kind of just a telephone friend. You know, if they're a cheap cab ride or they're one stop off the subway then they're a friend, but if they're past that then they're just a telephone friend, I guess.

CLIFTON – New York

Keeping in touch Keeping in contact with others becomes particularly important when the exigencies of city life restrict our ability to see friends and family. The way we do this when we cannot meet is via the telephone. The critical function of the telephone is not only to make appointments, pass messages and practical information, but to retain and maintain friendships. Frequently, this involves discussions about personal issues. Some issues are more easily discussed over the telephone than face to face, such as breaking appointments or passing on unwelcome messages. Breaking up is not so hard to do over the telephone.

As we have seen, the contribution of non-verbal cues makes face-to-face interactions extremely rich in comparison to any communication that does not involve visual information such as the telephone. This difference means that telephone talk differs in a number of ways from face-to-face conversations. This can have a number of advantages. It allows people to deal with difficult emotional issues without a direct confrontation. It is easier to use the telephone to end a relationship, although it is often regarded as cowardly because one doesn't have to see the emotional response and negotiate a way to leave the environment. The telephone also allows anonymity so making a complaint about something or behaving with extreme emotion does not lead to a full disclosure of identity. City dwellers have become particularly skilled at using the telephone to their advantage.

Even on the telephone we are able to present ourselves in particular ways. We adjust our voices according to those with whom we are speaking even though we cannot see them. When people are asked to judge the a recording of one side of a telephone conversation, they are able to identify systematic differences according to who the other party is. In many cases we deliberately alter our voices to appear, for example, more competent if talking to our boss or more relaxed if talking to a child or spouse.

Gossip Another way in which friendship and groups are maintained is by exchanging information about others – often on the telephone. Gossip is a crucial form of maintaining relationships. At best, it describes an easy-going and unconstrained form of conversation which essentially passes on information about others. First, gossip enables us to get information, to find out about people without having to ask them directly, therefore avoiding potential embarrassment to either party. Sharing gossip about others is one way of checking the reliability of information received. Gossip also provides an indirect way of obtaining information in order to understand others and make comparisons to oneself. By learning how others behave, we can evaluate our own actions.

In this way, gossip has a second important function of keeping group values and behaviours known and shared, even when face-to-face contact is infrequent. By talking to others, we are able to learn which behaviours, achievements and transgressions are acceptable or reasonable – or not – in the group to which we belong. In doing so, gossip influences the behaviour of others. A third function of gossip is that it is simply a form of entertainment. Entertainment gossip is engaged in primarily for personal amusement and satisfaction. It is guided by the principle of reciprocity in which the interacting parties are mutually benefited by exchanging stories and information about others with one another.

Phone obedience The very convenience of the telephone and the adoption of a tele-

TELEPHONE VS FACE-TO-FACE COMMUNICATION

I prefer to talk to people who aren't friends on the phone. If I'm booking a dentist appointment or cancelling it or something or trying to get say an extension on an essay or something, I'd rather talk to my tutor on the phone than face to face. And also people you're not too fond of, they don't know you're not too fond of them. It's any emotion, like if you're nervous, if it's somebody you don't really know very well, or you're bored, or scared of somebody or intimidated in any way . . . that's just one of many emotions that you can hide. I'm not very good at hiding things with my face. Which is a bit dishonest, I suppose.

CLARE – London

It's easier to quit jobs on the telephone. It's easier to fake being sick on the telephone. And [to] tell people you don't want to see them over the phone is a lot easier than staring somebody in the face and saying: 'I really don't want to hang out with you tonight.' So definitely I use that to my advantage.

KENYA – Los Angeles

Sometimes when you're on the phone and you're really mad at the other person, and because they're a customer or if they're a client you really can't show it to them. You can put yourself on mute or you can get off the phone and I'll hit the wall, or do something to release energy. But at least the person doesn't see it, they don't feel it, and that's the kind of nice thing about the phone.

DAVE – Los Angeles

The phone allows you to reinvent yourself. You can kind of be and project what you want over the phone. You're having a bad day for two minutes, you can pull it together and get on the phone and convey what you have to convey. In a big city it actually works to your advantage, because you can basically be and project what you want for whatever time you're on the phone, which is a great convenience here, because it's hard if people were to see you in every hour of your day.

ERROL – Los Angeles

phone culture ironically also make the city dweller a slave to this form of technology. Ever adaptable, however, *homo urbanus* has devized a solution which reasserts control over this particular machine: the answer phone and voice mail.

The answer phone has become one of the most widely used forms of new technology. At first it was resisted, but now has become widely used and accepted. Initially, its main function was to capture calls and contacts while someone was away from the telephone. But more recently, it is being used not only to capture calls but screen them. This enables us to respond to particular calls at our own convenience or even to choose not to respond. Generally, this is another form of time rescheduling that modern city dwellers use to assert control over their lives. Instead of doing things on demand or missing calls altogether, they can do it in their own time.

Increasingly, the telecommunications industry is devising a range of new mechanisms to increase the functions of the telephone and our ability to control that part of our life which relies on it. We can now know the number of callers to screen out nuisance calls, ranging from the garrulous friend to the more traumatic heavy breather. We have a call-waiting system which tells us when someone is trying to call us. This gives us the control to continue with the current conversation and ignore the incoming call, to switch to the new call, or to find out who is on the second call and then decide who to talk to. No longer do we have to be concerned about people calling us when we are visiting as we can divert our calls to wherever we want, including to an answer machine or voice mail. All these development keep us more in contact and embed telephone contact and communication into our lives.

Mobile phones   Studies show that individuals at work spend on average 20 per cent of time away from their desk or immediate work area. Four out of five telephone calls fail to get through because someone is either away from their desk or engaged. This led to the view that there was a need for a roving telephone that could be taken with you. Ironically, it is estimated the majority of calls that do get through are less important than the work they interrupt.

Nonetheless, the cordless phone became the telephone you could carry around in your pocket when walking about the office or home. The popularity of the cordless phone indicated that city dwellers wanted mobility in their telecommunications. The majority of all telephones purchased in the United States are now cordless, and over one-third of all American homes has a cordless telephone. But if you could move about the office and home with your telephone, then why not the garden, the street or the next city? Almost as soon as it was developed, the cordless telephone did not offer enough range, and the mobile phone was born.

The number of mobile telephones in use in 1994 was estimated as 40 million. North America, Asia and Europe account for 95 per cent of all users.

In China the number of mobile telephones increased from 20,000 in 1990 to 1.57 million in 1994. With the increased use it is estimated that by the year 2000 there will be between 150 and 250 million mobile telephones.

The United States has the single largest market with 15 million users in 1994. It is estimated that this will rise to 60 million in 2000. From only about one in seventeen of the population (6 per cent) having a mobile telephone in 1994, more than one in five Americans (20 per cent) are expected to have them by the year 2000.

In Hong Kong and Singapore, one in twenty people (5 per cent) have mobile telephones, and in Scandinavia, more than one in ten (10 per cent) will shortly have one.

In addition to mobile telephones, pagers are also widely used for keeping people in contact. It is estimated that pagers will be used by 100 to 120 million by 2000. Already 24 million are used in China.

Being able to be in contact at all times in all places is the watchword of fast city living. Although the mobile telephone and pager were originally sold as business tools, they have now permeated into everyday use. The majority of users of mobile telephones – 58 per cent in 1994 – are now domestic.

The main reasons why people purchase mobile telephones are the mobility it provides and the perceived increase in productivity and flexibility in business. Freedom and flexibility are probably the most important attractions. Originally, the main reason for purchasing a mobile telephones was to facilitate both business and friendly calls. Today, the dominant reason for new purchasers is safety. In fact, safety is one of the main marketing devices used by mobile phone sellers. It is difficult to say which came first, the individual's fear for their safety or a shrewd selling strategy which recognized a new market for the mobile telephone among women in particular. What is important is that although the mobile phone may have been purchased for safety it soon becomes a general tool for communication.

MOBILE PHONES

I have a cellphone that was initially intended only for emergency use, but I think the definition of emergency has been relaxed. I'm on my cellphone too much. If I'm running late or if I need to talk to somebody and I can't leave the classroom, then I'll put my kids to work writing an essay and I'll poke my head in this little closet [and use the cellphone].

KATH – Los Angeles

Other communication technologies

The internet Computers have added to the myriad of ways in which we communicate. E-mail and the internet have allowed us to communicate cheaply and easily with one another. But they have removed yet another layer of intimacy from our interactions.

There has been a logarithmic increase in the use of, and access to, the internet. It was estimated to reach over 30 million individuals by 1993 and has spread to 127 countries around the world.

This form of new technology requires the mastery of a range of new skills. The content and timing of the exchanges is considerably different to voice communication. The loss of non-verbal cues which often accompany verbal information is a critical difference, particularly if they help in understanding the motives and underlying sentiments of those with whom we communicate, as many believe they do.

In general, when people are asked about their favoured means of communication within an office, they currently rank face-to-face contact first, then telephone communications highest, followed by meetings, desktop video and video conferencing, voice mail, text, and finally electronic mail. The key dimension to their preferences appears to be the simultaneous nature of the more face-to-face communication, and the fact that it provides them with other personal information. Although electronic mail is construed as being similar on some dimensions to written activities such as note writing – for example, its asynchrony and emotional quality – it is sometimes rated as similar to spoken, face-to-face communication on other dimensions such as spontaneity.

The low ranking of electronic mail may have something to do with people's reliance on, and lack of, technical support within their organizations. A study comparing voice and electronic mail found that employees' preferences for the latter were related to their computer skills, the ease with which they could use their electronic mail system, and the support in the organization for electronic mail.

The advantages of e-mail Many users, however, see the heightened anonymity of the computer screen as having hidden advantages. For obvious reasons of privacy, few studies have been made of the content of electronic mail messages, even though there is a suggestion that it has become the favoured means of communication used by international drug traffickers.

Communications technologies have increased exponentially in recent years and the vast network of different types characterises the modern world as almost nothing else does.

One study examined the contents of students' electronic mail messages. Students are an interesting group, as they can use electronic mail in most cases unhindered by the costs, because it is free at the point of use within universities. In this study, over a six-month period, less than half the electronic mail messages of the 700 undergraduate subjects addressed work-related concerns. For the most part, electronic mail served a purely social function, with about a quarter of all messages containing intimate content. Few messages conveyed hostility or were judged to be socially inappropriate.

The influence of social status is considerably different in face-to-face communication as opposed to that done through electronic mail. Research has found electronic mail to be a great leveller. A study of decision-making, comparing the process when people met in person to when they used electronic mail, found large differences. When groups of people made decisions in face-to-face meetings, the high-status members tended to dominate the discussion. They were also more likely to be the first advocate of a solution in the discussion. (In general, first advocates tend to be more influential than later advocates in decision-making.) When the same groups made comparable decisions using electronic mail, the status differences were reduced. The internet extends the equality of the electronic network, in that in theory, anybody can address anybody else on the net. There are no difficulties in directing communications to anyone, and social standing in this public world is no barrier to access.

Although communication by electronic mail is considerably different to face-to-face communication, a separate issue relates to whether the behaviour of people communicating via the net is different to that of people with face-to-face contact. A study looking at the group behaviour of individuals communicating electronically within a company showed they behaved like any other social group, despite the fact that the normal context for group behaviour was absent: they shared no physical space, were invisible to each other, and had asynchronous interactions (that is, there was some time between their interactions with each other.

Electronic mail is now seen as a substitute for, and an extension to, face-to-face communication. Some people spend more time interacting with their computer terminals than they do in face-to-face communication. But social interaction on the internet requires a different set of rules and offers new opportunities.

Cyberworld There are a number of specific dimensions that characterize the relative anonymity of computer communications over the internet. We do not have any information about the social context of the person with whom we are communicating; we know nothing of their social status. What is interesting is that many people on the internet wish to remain anonymous. Simple information such as the gender of the person we are communicating with is not necessarily available. This has led some to argue that the computer is neutral.

However, what it does is to allow someone to pretend to be somebody else, a member of the opposite sex, of a different age, or having different interests. Essentially the computer allows people to choose an identity, masquerade as someone else, or even adopt a number of different characters. The computer enables gender change without cross dressing or an operation. The anonymity of the city is extended by the anonymity of the internet. The stage of the internet allows many more costumes to be worn and roles to be played.

Netiquette Unlike the system of face-to-face communication where we have, in any culture, a set of deeply ingrained rules governing the
etiquette of communication, the conventions of the internet are not as well developed. The new manuals for using the internet now are attempting to develop a 'netiquette' by printing rules for using the net. For example, some managers of systems will expel people for using abusive language (known as flaming) or pretending to be someone of the opposite sex. Policing this last behaviour is only possible in limited networks where users are well known or when they can be found out.

In face-to-face communication we use both linguistic and non-verbal cues to give emotional feedback on our response to what is being said. In computer communications there are no visual and non-verbal cues, and in addition there are no supralinguistic cues of tone or intonation. The inability to convey emotions in this way, such as expressions of joy, approval and friendship amongst others, is a significant deficiency of communicating over the internet.

This limitation of the net and the need to have some way of communicating emotion was recognized as an important limitation of computer communication. Early in the development of the internet, people developed signs and symbols to be used to communicate emotion and expressions, in order to substitute and extend the medium to make it more like face-to-face communication. There are a number of examples of systems of symbols and many are now in common use. Some

SOME EXAMPLES OF NETIQUETTE

Do not answer a message in anger! If you are provoked, stay cool a few hours before you answer.

Be proud of the message. Never send anything you will regret later.

Never write anything you would not say to the recipient in a face-to-face situation with others present.

:-)	A basic smile	;-)	A smiling face and a winking eye
:-X	A big wet kiss	:-(	A sour face
:-(*)	Feeling sick	:-P	Pointing the tongue
:-O	A scream	=8-(	A horrified face with wide open eyes
i>	Irony	}—\——-.---	A rose, token of love

electronic groups have been found to use up to a hundred of these. These symbols go a little way to replacing the visual and verbal clues that have been lost.

Meeting on the net The internet has established its meeting system with people using the net as a meeting place. The use of bulletin boards for meeting people is now widespread and some are coupled with photographs. This provides important visual information about the corre-spondent. The advertisements are similar to those found in newspapers, but once again the medium enables individuals to cross physical boundaries and seek partners or relationships at a much greater distance.

The internet extends the variety of techniques people use to meet in the city. Communication groups are ordered into areas of interest and participants are able to join groups and join discussions, raise issues, and meet others with shared interests without the constraint of geographical proximity. The internet provides the modern medium with millions of potential friends available for contact. The internet allows people to build up social networks and friendships, and romances have even developed over it.

Although covering 30 million people, this medium has not spread, like the telephone, where most people have access to the technology from their homes. Both the expense as well as knowledge and skill have restricted the spread of access to electronic mail. The ever resourceful city, however, has attempted to bridge the gap with the growth of internet cafes and bars, where people can access the internet for a period of time but do not have to face the financial outlay of acquiring all the equipment. These public internet access locations also allow users of the internet to meet and exchange information.

Teleshopping Another area where new technology will have a considerable impact on the decline in direct face-to-face contacts in the future involves being able to shop directly over the television. Although television shopping is widely available in the United States, it still tends not to have the flexibility that modern teleshopping will introduce in the long term.

Two factors associated with the benefits of direct shopping appear to influence whether people adopt teleshopping. First, the direct experience of the store or shopping-mall environment is currently considered superior in terms of information quality and quantity to that obtained through teleshopping for many products. The degree of uncertainty about purchasing a product is often influenced by being able to handle the goods. In addition, store shopping serves more than simply the acquisition of goods and products. It offers both recreation and social contacts that are currently not possible when teleshopping. (The importance of shopping and its role as one of the most dominant behaviours in the city is discussed in Chapter 6.)

Shopping may be the last area to succumb to the technology revolution because of its multiple functions, but as the generation who have learned to use the internet while at school grow up, they may be more likely to make the switch to teleshopping. We are still learning to adapt to these new technologies. Although they allow us to form new types of communities, they have the potential to isolate us still further from those people immediately around us.

A PERSONAL AD ON THE NET

Of course one of the easiest people to meet on the net is ME. This is particularly significant if you are a tall, single, outgoing, open minded, FEMALE, oh say between 21 and 30, you thought the picture you saw of me on the way in here was kind of cute and you're reasonably close to Cincinnati, willing to relocate to Cincinnati, or can point me in the direction of a $10/hr job in a part of the country where a reasonable nice 1BR apartment is in the $400/mo range. You can contact me by e-mail . . .

Chapter 4

Making Sense of the World

I cursed the people who have the kind of brains to create these machines. You don't know if it's not working because you've used the wrong socket or whether you've actually broken it or ripped a cable by mistake or even made the thing explode silently but deadly inside. There's no light that flashes and says 'well done' or 'yes' or 'no' when you've got it right. And then you switch it on and there's a blank screen or a snow storm on the screen. It's like a kind of maze.

ANASTASIA – London

Knowing the city

It is easy to feel confused in the modern world. Everywhere we go in the city we are bombarded with a dazzling array of things to make sense of. In order to function efficiently in any city, we need knowledge. Part of that knowledge is the crucial ability to find your way around. Those who can find their way around are usually more experienced in city living. Newcomers have to master a very complex and often confusing layout of buildings, streets, and intersections, the rationale for which is not always obvious at first sight. To survive, newcomers must learn quickly how to get from one place to another. One group for whom this has real meaning are city taxi drivers who need to be able to take their customers to innumerable destinations. 'Doing the knowledge' is a familiar term, referring to London taxi drivers' need to master the warren of streets and routes before getting their licences to practise.

Some cities are easier than others to negotiate. The inherent complexity of all the activity going on within a city, as well as the way in which it is configured, influences the ease with which we can find our way around. Many North American cities, for instance, although highly complex, are organized on the basis of a grid in which street names are numbered. This allegedly makes it simpler to move about, although some would argue that the simplicity gained is at the cost of cultural and historical markers. The configuration of a city refers to the way in which its different parts and locations of the city relate to each other.

Spatial knowledge is complex and contains at least two kinds of information. One is information about a relationship between two objects, known as 'propositional knowledge'. An example of this is being aware that Boston is north of New York. Another is information about the length or range between places, known as 'spatial knowledge'. An example is knowing how far apart places are on a map. Most of the problems we face in the city involve judgements about these two things, orientation (propositional knowledge) and distance (spatial knowledge), as well as routes linking one place to another.

Finding our way around.

Mental maps Finding our way in the city is a feat of ingenuity. But for those who are familiar with an area this becomes such second nature that they hardly appear to stop and think. This is because we all carry our own personal map of the city in our heads, telling us which directions to take, how long the journey is or what short cuts are available. A popular way of demonstrating mental maps is to ask someone to count the number of windows in their house. For most people this involves mentally walking through their house, counting the windows as they go.

In order to make sense of the city, we create images or cognitions of its geography in our head. This activity is accompanied by physiological changes. When we create an image, blood flow increases to the visual areas of the brain. This blood flow reflects increased activity in the visual cortex as we produce the mental image.

The strength of the argument that we use some form of mental image or representation comes from a study in which students were asked to estimate the distance between familiar locations on their university campus. They took more time estimating long distances than short distances, as if they were mentally walking through or measuring the distance between the points in their heads. It clearly takes longer to do this when the mental distances are further apart.

We can all create an image in our heads of the downtown area of the city we live in. These mental maps of our worlds are an important way in which we understand and respond to the complexities of the urban environment. They are built up by our experience in the world and our use of standard maps for finding our way around. According to Kevin Lynch, who developed the concept of a mental map, they consist of a number of features which include 'paths' that we use to move along, 'nodes' where we find a convergence of paths, 'landmarks' which are physically distinctive objects such as an exceptional building, and 'boundaries' or 'edges' of areas which mark the shift from one 'territory' or 'district' to another.

Creating mental maps Two views exist of how we create mental maps. One maintains that the creation of paths or routes between places is the first step in producing mental maps of cities. According to this view, when first generating a mental map, most people tend to assemble the routes they use and position landmarks on these routes. They then build up a representation of the boundaries and districts. These are combined together to finish up with the overall mental map. This view implies that we construct mental maps from our experience in traversing the city, and once we know the routes we place landmarks into our mental maps.

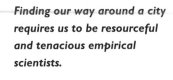

Finding our way around a city requires us to be resourceful and tenacious empirical scientists.

In order to make sense of the city we create images of its geography in our heads.

An alternative view suggests that in the first stage of constructing a mental map of the city we use landmarks, again based on our experience. Only after we have these landmarks do we fill in routes between them. By this view we begin to create our mental maps with landmarks and then link them by means of routes.

Whichever system is used to create mental maps – routes followed by landmarks or landmarks followed by routes, or even a combination of the two – we proceed to cluster the routes together in an integrated fashion. In the final stage, we have a mental representation of the survey map which combines landmarks and routes into a pattern. Remarkably, if we draw this representation, the distances between landmarks are correct relative to one another, even though we may never have walked them.

The importance of a mental map is that it is a structure where routes and landmarks can be related to each other, much like a survey map. This enables us to cover some routes between landmarks that we have not been on before. What we do is to use our knowledge of the overall

London was just a series of tube stops. You don't actually realize how close they all are. You think that they're miles apart, but after you've done London quite a few times, you get to realize how close things are: the tourist areas are in one area, like Leicester Square and everything else, and then business areas are in another area. After a while it becomes clearer. You work out how and where everything inter-connects with each other, and it's not just a series of stops on the Underground.

CLARE – London

I try to find the roads back to my place. That takes time, finding the landmarks. I pick landmarks and places where I go, so I can easily come back home most of the time.

DANIEL – Los Angeles

Well, I guess I have different kinds of mental maps to this city. There's the shopping map, with core shopping areas; then there's the restaurant map; then there would be the nightclub or the lounge map. There's a friend map, where different friends of mine are spread out through the city . . . and an ex-boyfriend map – no, not really, I'm kidding.

KATH – Los Angeles

relationships between routes, landmarks and orientation to judge how we can make a connection between two landmarks by moving in particular directions. The great usefulness of this mental representation is that it enables us to problem solve in the city.

After some time, we build up a flexible, albeit incomplete, mental representation of the city. In fact, what we arrive at is a detailed mental picture of the area in which most of our activity is based. We then tend to have fingers or branches going out from our local areas to particular destinations on the periphery, or sometimes to even more distant places from our centre. We know the routes to and from these destinations, but often know little about what happens in between them.

The development of our mental maps continually evolves. In the initial phases of life in the city, it may take months or even years to develop an accuracy and level of completeness. In some senses, our maps can never be complete because we continually update them as buildings change, and routes redirected.

The amount of information that professionals, such as taxi drivers, have to remember is enormous. The principles on which their mental maps are based are the same as regular city dwellers, but it is not surprising to discover their mental maps are somewhat more complex. Studies of Parisian taxi drivers show they have two levels of mental mapping which complement each other. They have excellent knowledge of a 'basic network' which reflects the major arteries and intersections of the city. This contains about 10 per cent of the roads. When they use this basic network, they are extremely accurate at estimating distances and using it to select optimal routes. The 'secondary network' has a direct relationship to the basic network in that it fits onto it. But, secondary networks do not relate to each other. So taxi drivers pick up a fare, use their secondary network to move to their basic network, progress along the basic network until they get close to the destination, and then invoke another secondary network to complete the trip.

We tend to have some difficulty in altering our mental maps once we have formed them. When we use routes regularly they tend to be built into our maps very strongly and reflect our behaviour. So, for example, once we have established a route to and from work, many of us tend to stick to that route, even in the face of additional information about alternative routes. This habitual behaviour restricts the efficiency with which city dwellers move around their city. Flexibility both in developing a mental map and in behaviour is the key to working effectively for some groups like messengers, taxi drivers, and police who need to move through the city quickly and efficiently. Taxi drivers also need to keep up with road works and road closures and therefore, often have a range of alternative routes available.

Cities vary in the extent to which they lend themselves to the creation of mental maps; they differ in their 'legibility'. In some cities a prominent feature such as a mountain or the sea act to improve legibility. A city such as Cape Town, which is built around a mountain and where someone can always orient themself in relation to the mountain, has greatly assisted legibility. Manhattan has a grid-like street structure which aids legibility, but the high-rise buildings obscure the view making it more difficult to orient oneself. London has a river which aids legibility but the fact that streets curve and wind make it difficult to produce an accurate mental map.

Equally importantly, people's mental maps differ considerably from one another. As may be expected if mental maps are constructed through experience, what someone does influences which landmarks they adopt, what paths they use, and the importance of different areas. For instance, the mental maps of older people are smaller and more highly localized, reflecting their lower levels of mobility.

Landmarks Landmarks are presumed to act as a kind of anchor point for our knowledge of the city. Several different aspects of the urban environment can act as a landmark. For some

Buildings become anchor points and landmarks for our spatial knowledge of the city.

one unfamiliar with a city, it may be restricted to a large building, fountain or sculpture. For others who are familiar with the environment, the landmark may be a small aspect of a building like a particular door.

We may also define a building as a landmark by its function, such as a police station or post office, or by its appearance. Something that might be a significant landmark to one person may remain completely unnoticed by another. Certain features make a building more salient and increase its likelihood of being used as a landmark. Two obvious examples of this are the height and shape of a building. But less evident characteristics such as the number of people moving around it and the degree of maintenance will also influence its likelihood of being adopted.

Distortions   The maps we carry in our heads are individualistic and represent only a part of the world we live in. They are also simplifications of this world. More importantly, they distort reality. This is epitomized by the map of New York – used by the New Yorker magazine to illustrate how New Yorkers view the United States – which has spawned a whole host of imitators.

One consistent distortion or error we make in mentally judging the distance between two points is that the more intervening places there are between the two points, the longer we estimate the distance to be. So, if asked to judge the length between two points, along which there are few barriers to be crossed, we would judge it to be shorter than if we were thinking about a busy environment where there were many objects and barriers. We also distort distance if a slope is involved. If an area we walk along contains either an upward or a downward slope, we tend to overestimate how far it is. This also happens in relation to routes consisting of stairs and those that are curved rather than straight. It appears as though we take into account effort as well as length, and psychological rather than actual distance.

We tend to simplify maps in interesting ways. A common one is to make curves straight. When Parisians were asked to draw the map they had in their heads for Paris, over 90 per cent underestimated the curvature of the Seine. This led to significant distortions of their overall image of Paris. We also simplify by making all angled intersections into right angles. Los Angeles residents can draw the downtown grid area of Los Angeles with some degree of accuracy because its street crossings tend to be at 90 degrees. On the other hand, they systematically distort more irregular out-of-town areas by incorrectly making those intersections into right angles. When people are taken on a route they are inclined to move by default in a right-angled direction. If, for instance, they walk a route which has signs giving directions, they tend to exaggerate the turns that need to be made between 0 and 90 degrees and discount those between 90 and 180 degrees. In other words, they typically tend to take right-angled turns.

A further way we distort our learning is through experience. When we walk through the city we see a range of buildings. These are often physically organized to some degree into groups, with furniture stores clustered in one district and electronics stores in another. This general understanding of how many cities are organized leads us to a distortion in our mental maps. What we tend to do is to group the different types of stores closer together than they actually are. This process is emphasized when we learn that different districts have different names. What we are doing in our minds is to move particular buildings closer to those districts so they fit in with the categories we have in our understanding of the city.

·Personal preferences determine some aspects of our mental maps. When we don't like a location, for whatever reason, we conveniently decide it is further away than it really is. Locations we do like we deem to be closer. Urban residents, who associate the urban area with pleasure and satisfaction, tend to judge movements into the city centre as closer than movements out of it. The emotional reactions we have to places and how they distort our judgements of distance are particularly salient in relation to newcomers, and appear to decline with time.

As we have seen, the maps we have in our heads are not realistic in their shape or scale. They are individual and egocentric, distorted to suit ourselves and the task they need to perform.

Street maps Learning and using both formal and informal street maps is an integral part of city life. The work of some people such as taxi drivers, delivery men and women, and the police, is critically dependent upon maps. Some argue that a person cannot build up a true survey-type mental map from experience alone. These theorists maintain that we need exposure to real survey maps. Others argue that true mental maps are constructed from experience alone. Whichever view is correct, the question remains as to whether a real survey map aids our understanding of a city. For many visitors, the real survey map of a city is an important first step in the development of a mental map, and they often consult these maps before entering a city.

The importance of designing a survey map for newcomers to the city is something faced by most tourist agencies. When people are asked what kind of survey maps they like, they report a preference for maps with landmarks and distances. Many maps of cities include landmarks often as drawings of buildings. It is unclear whether these kinds of maps, in contrast to standard street-only maps, influence the ability to move between locations. This is particularly important for drivers, as landmarks on maps may be more difficult to discern from a car than when walking. Survey-map learning and transferring this knowledge into the real world is a demanding task.

On entering a new city, it is common for us to use a survey map, linking it to our experience of walking or travelling through the city. Learning from maps and learning from experience are different. Learning from survey maps seems to be linked to the orientation in which the learning occurs. If someone looks at the map from one orientation it is sometimes difficult to use the information when approaching from a different orientation. This can be seen when travelling in a car or even walking by means of a map: many people rotate it when they come to junctions where routes cross, in order to determine which way to go. People who have studied a map and are then asked for directions, are also more accurate when the directional questions relate to the orientation in which they learned the map. Having to mentally rotate the map in our head is a difficult process and can cause

some errors. Learning from experience does not limit the understanding gained to a particular orientation and seems to provide greater flexibility. When someone has learned from experience the need to rotate does not seem to be as difficult.

Many city dwellers are used to the common experience of giving visitors or even other city people instructions on how to get to particular locations, especially in big cities where it is impossible to be familiar with the complete layout of the city. These directions, or more accurately descriptions, commonly include a series of landmarks and then instructions to get from one landmark to another. Studies comparing instructions given to a driver verbally, by means of a map, or by a combination of map and verbal instructions, show that drivers make fewer errors and spend less time driving when they are given verbal instructions only. The addition of a map did not improve their efforts at navigation. This suggests that some

Using street maps helps us to understand complex urban environments and aids the formation of our mental maps.

mental mapping of a particular route given verbally can be even more efficient than using a real map.

Inside buildings   Cities are characterized by large, often complicated buildings which we also have to be able to negotiate. A good example of this is the multi-storey shopping centre or entertainment complex. The uniform symmetry of these buildings may be aesthetically pleasing, but it makes one direction look much like another. To move easily through buildings such as these requires a map of the layout, some kind of mental representation of the interior design of the building: a mental map of the building.

In the same way that cities differ in the extent to which they lend themselves to making mental maps, so do buildings. Some are intrinsically more difficult to decipher than others. In fact, some buildings have developed a reputation for being difficult to negotiate. A classic example of this is the major arts complex in London, known as the Barbican Centre, which has 20 to 30 million visitors per year.

The complexity of a floor plan is the most important factor which determines whether it is easy or difficult for someone to find their way around an environment such as this. The floor plan of the Barbican Centre is particularly difficult to interpret, first, because entry to the building is at the middle level, and second, because people then have to move down followed by moving up some stairs in order to stay on the same level. This seems to be disorienting because it goes against expectations or common sense. The Barbican developed a culture of being lost.

Recently, a whole new system has been introduced to make it easier for people to find their way around. This includes re-numbering floors so that the entry floor at ground level was labelled 0 and the floors below had negative numbers (-1, -2 etc) and the floors above were numbered positively. New signs were introduced which also named the activity which occurred on the floors. A walkway was introduced so that people were able to keep on the same level when moving from the main entrance rather than going up and down staircases. In addition, carpets were coloured for each floor. As might be expected, people who can find their way around shopping malls or museums report higher levels of satisfaction with their visit than people who have difficulty finding their way around.

Floor plans   Providing a floor plan, or 'you are here' map, on various walls has become one of the most common ways in which architects and planners provide the public with the general layout of a building, and an idea of both where they are and where they might wish to go. Floor plans are especially important when it is not possible to see the layout of a building. A common problem is how they are aligned. When the 'you are here'

arrow is upright and appropriate to the viewer's position, they tend to be more accurate. When they have to be rotated, as with any map, they cause difficulties and this seems to be especially so for older individuals. The misaligned floor plan or map is more difficult to read and interpret because we have to make an additional mental calculation in order to take the correct direction.

In some buildings, people are given a map which is designed to supplement the floor plans, notices and maps posted around the building. These hand-out maps have been shown to be very effective in familiarizing visitors with art galleries and museums, and when well designed, are almost always used by people visiting public buildings. They are the main technique people use for finding their way around.

The design of buildings encourages people to move through some areas more than others. This means our behaviour in moving around buildings is not random. We also bring with us an understanding, from our previous experience, of how buildings in general are organized. For example, we expect an entrance to lead into a hallway or vestibule, and then to be faced with the choice of alternative directions which will include the possibility of going upstairs or on a level plane.

Architects and planners, with varying degrees of success, try to assist city dwellers and especially newcomers to find their way around. Sign systems are widely used to do this inside and outside builidngs. Signs introduced at specific points where choices must be made about routes, significantly improve people's ability to negotiate the building. The evidence suggests that graphic signs or illustrations are more effective at helping people than written signs. One study showed that in five different settings, graphic signs increased people's ability to move quickly through a building, halved the number of wrong turns they made, and reduced the amount of backtracking they had to do by about two-thirds.

Colour is another technique widely used to assist people routing themselves. When walls are painted a uniform colour throughout a building, finding the way around becomes more difficult. When colour systems are introduced to indicate different areas of the building, people are found to make fewer errors.

Different levels in shopping centres add a vertical dimension to mental mapping. Finding our way about on two dimensions in the city is difficult enough; doing so on three dimensions adds considerably to the complexity. Moving through shopping malls can be particularly confusing as there are no external landmarks.

Getting lost

Getting lost and confused in a city can cause enormous stress. Trying to find the way around a city on two dimensions is difficult enough. But the introduction of a vertical dimension, creating a movement through three-dimensional space, adds considerably to the difficulty. This happens, for instance, in large shopping centres. For many people the name of shops are used to locate a place. Nonetheless, the errors that tend to be made are ones on the vertical dimension, because many shops whose names are used as landmarks extend vertically over more than one storey. This can be baffling, particularly for relative newcomers.

The most common time when people become disoriented in a city is when they leave an underground train station. This is not surprising, because the movement between locations in the underground provides no visual clues to where you actually are in the city.

GETTING LOST

When I get lost in the Galleria, I look up and see what stores are familiar, and I know that at one end there is a large department store and at the other end there's another one. If I see Broadway I know that I have to go the other way, because I generally walk out or walk in by way of Penny's. So that gives me an idea of where I am. But when you're just standing there and you can't look and all you see are stores and people, you're really bewildered.

RONNIE – Los Angeles

Shopping

Fortunately, we are tailored to make sense of the world around us. When we're shopping, one of the most important predictors of where we shop is whether we have been there before. Familiarity reduces the effort that has to be made because it enables us to find what we want to buy more quickly. Many people set out with shopping strategies. They plan in advance the sequence they will travel, which shops they will visit, and roughly how long the trip will take. By returning to a familiar environment we are able to reduce the load of information that we have to process when shopping.

Supermarket shopping Shopping in a supermarket presents us with a complex locating task. We have a clear idea that we want some particular objects, some general objects, but we also want to browse to see what is on the shelves. Nonetheless, we are frequently on a tight time line and have to complete the shopping quickly. By frequently patronizing a

We search for the objects we want in a supermarket by scanning the shelves using our peripheral vision.

shop we can recall store layout and quickly find the goods we want. The extent to which we rely on this in our busy city lives is evidenced by the confusion and frustration that ensues when goods are moved around. Sometimes this is done by managers as a strategy to keep customers longer in the store on the assumption that they will buy more the longer they have to move around, and see things they had not thought of buying at the outset.

It is incorrect to assume the shopper who has an idea of the object they wish to buy, proceeds straightforwardly with their initial plan. Take for example the situation of shopping for a toothbrush in a supermarket. Although someone may be used to a particular brand and fully intends to look for that brand, the supermarket shelves present an enormous array of different toothbrushes, in different colours, with different packaging and often with different special offers. When all these options are presented, the shopper may reassess both their needs and their wants. In some cases, they may choose to switch brands to see what the other brand is like.

Going shopping with others influences our behaviour. When we go

Going shopping with others influences our behaviour and choice of product. Supermarkets know that children are attracted to certain goods and are careful to place them where they can easily be seen.

shopping in a group with other people, we tend to stay in the shop longer and to purchase more. Having others with us changes the nature of the shopping trip. It often leads us to make more purchases except if the purchase is personal, when we are likely to be inhibited. But in general, as with other behaviours, having others around encourages us in our shopping behaviour.

Another important finding indicates that, whatever we may like to believe, much of our shopping behaviour is unplanned and we make a considerable number of spontaneous purchases. Impulse buying is a large component of purchasing in all types of shopping. Overall, it is estimated to account for just under one-third of all purchases. In the supermarket, impulse buying is even higher, accounting for the remarkable figure of up to half of grocery purchases.

How we choose   When we enter a typical supermarket we are confronted with about 20,000 different items. From all these items we may wish to select only about twenty or thirty. The task for us as shoppers is to

We don't often know exactly what we want when we go shopping. The displays tempt us to buy things we never intended. Over half our purchases in the supermarket are estimated to be bought on impulse.

move through the supermarket, search the shelves generally for the items we want, and then select a particular product from the general type of item we are seeking. This involves us in a search process and, as with many of our activities, we have to deal with an enormous clutter of objects. How we visually search objects and how we move down shopping aisles is in fact a complex process.

When we walk down a shopping aisle we are normally doing a number of things besides scanning the shelves. We are pushing a trolley, negotiating it so that it doesn't bang into others, and if we are with others, are either talking or controlling and organizing children.

Scanning is the most interesting behaviour. To understand it, we must distinguish between that which happens at our central vision where we are able to perform a detailed analysis of objects, and our peripheral vision where much of the search activity takes place. In theory, using our peripheral vision, we can scan up to 180 degrees horizontally and 120 degrees vertically. But when we consider the area we can usefully use in peripheral vision, in ideal circumstances, it extends about 60 degrees horizontally before we make any eye movements (30 degrees on either side). With eye movements the effective range increases to 80 degrees. To extend beyond that we need to use head movements. It is from this field of vision that we can usefully extract information. The importance of peripheral vision can be appreciated from the fact that we spend most of our time in the supermarket not looking at the products on the shelves. We only look directly at the products on display for about 40 per cent of the time.

When we walk down a supermarket aisle, therefore, we automatically scan the shelves using our peripheral vision. This peripheral vision allows us to sample the objects on the shelves to see if they match what we are looking for. So we selectively filter out objects and shelves which don't fit in with what we are seeking. If we see the object in the periphery then we subject it to closer scrutiny. The process is complex because we are continually analysing the information sampled in our peripheral vision and comparing it to our mental image of the objects we are seeking, or weighing up whether the object interests us.

It has been demonstrated that we tend to use two types of scanning. In one, called 'passive scanning', the head is kept at a fixed angle of approximately 20 degrees to the products on display. At the same time, we are pushing a trolley down the aisle and so are using much of our vision on the task of negotiating while still scanning the merchandise. We also engage in 'active scanning', where we more actively look around the store, making head movements, in response to what attracts us in the store.

Colour enables us to search much more effectively. Size and shape are

New technology has some unexpected uses, enabling us to confirm what we need when shopping. It allows us to do two things at once, making us more efficient, and taking the boredom out of grocery shopping.

next in importance to colour as cues helping us to search for things. If we are looking for a jar of spread that we know has a particular brown colour, when we see a brown object we focus our central vision onto it. If it is clear that the object is the wrong shape, we will avert our gaze. The eye movements that take us to the object all happen in a fraction of a second. So we move almost imperceptibly down the aisle, making head and eye movements towards the shelves where appropriate. When we are in a domain which contains the general type of object we are looking for, we may subject a range of alternative objects to careful scrutiny.

Our search processes are influenced by the display. If the shelves are cluttered with all sorts of different goods, we feel overloaded and our useful area of vision will be narrowed. Our search process will be less efficient and we will be slower when scanning cluttered displays because we can only perceive a relatively small area of the shelf. Also, our scanning tends to be more accurate and sensitive in our search for objects on a horizontal plane.

We know the aspect of vision most easily detected in the periphery is movement. Having vertical lines on the shelves leads to a perception of movement (called vertical blocking) when walking down a supermarket aisle. So when we walk down an aisle which has vertical blocking we often glance towards the shelf because it is as if we have seen a movement in the periphery of our vision. This increases the likelihood that a display will be noticed. The technique is often used in supermarkets to indicate that the product or brand has changed.

The principles of visual search have been used by many supermarkets for some time in organizing their displays. They tend to use simple uncluttered displays, with similar products grouped together. They create vertical lines in displays to distinguish different products. They tend to place strong brands at eye level. Studies by Ray Bradshaw using hidden cameras have examined the likelihood of customers looking at products on a display and have shown they are more likely to do so when the display is simple, and has clear vertical lines between them. By making these changes in the display of items, supermarkets can increase shoppers' perceptions of objects enormously. A number of studies have shown that the likelihood of scanning the products increased fourfold, and viewing certain shelves doubled, as did recalling the objects that were on display. It takes only milliseconds to make mental judgements about deciding which purchases we will make. One might expect this to be a stressful experience, but in fact we achieve this complex task almost effortlessly.

Making sense of technology

In the modern city we are surrounded by tens of thousands of usable objects, from zips to staples, window latches to computer screens. Each requires a knowledge of how they operate. No matter how well equipped we think we might be, there is always some new gadget to make sense of.

Many people believe the amount of personal time available to them in their daily lives is shrinking, and that they are putting in more time at work than did their parents. When asked in a Gallup Poll, however, only 14 per cent of Americans said that they would sacrifice some income for more time; the job is the only aspect of many people's lives where time is considered sacrosanct. If this is generally true, then people will increasingly look for mechanisms and gadgets that can save them time.

However, all is not always well in the design of new technology and the ease with which it can be used. Modern household objects are marketed and sold with countless, often unnecessary functions. Instruction books can take hours to read and understand. In the end, most people never master all the alternatives on the household objects they buy and use.

Take, for example, the washing machine. There are three essential dimensions to a household washing machine. These are temperature, spin speed and number of cycles or washes. Most individuals rely on only three types of washes, despite most machines offering more than twelve.

Offering as many alternatives as possible is central to the marketing of these machines even when purchasers are left bemused by all the controls as well as the often unintelligible instruction manuals. Apart from whether we need all these alternative functions in everyday objects, there is also the issue of why it is that so many everyday objects are perceived to be confusing and difficult to use, when new technology was supposed to introduce convenience and ease of use into our lives.

Design hell The visual design of many household objects is often governed by the aesthetic and not ease of use. Donald Norman has argued strongly that one reason for the difficulty is the problem of design. Some objects contain visible clues as to their operations which help us understand their workings, while with others their operations are obscure and confusing. For example, the water tap in some showers is designed to provide a single action control for both heat and volume of water. This may be useful for someone who uses the same shower, but not for someone who moves in and out of hotel rooms which all have different systems. The most common way we find out how it works is by trial and error, because without a set of instructions, it is not obvious how to get the water to flow, let alone heat up.

It is critical in the design of an object that its separate parts clearly convey what they are to be used for. John Norman uses the example of a door. The vertical metal plate on the side of a door conveys the message that the hinge is on the other side and the door must be pushed at that point. These types of signals are referred to as 'natural signals'. They are natural because we interpret them with ease and they do not need complex signs to indicate their function. Natural designs incorporate natural signals and end up as articles that are easy to use.

Where the function that an object is designed to perform fits in with people's understanding of the object, then it is easy to use. Obvious examples of these are found everywhere: handles are for turning, buttons for pressing, keys for inserting, switches for turning, and so on. This relationship between function and understanding of an object (referred to as affordance) generally works well with simple objects. However, when we extend our world to complex objects such as video recorders, mobile phones and computers, the relationship between aspects of the object and their function becomes more remote and obscure.

The most interesting contrast in recent years is the computer design difference between the Apple Macintosh and the Personal Computer prior to the introduction of the Windows environment. For the Macintosh computer, the affordance was clearly laid out as the screen with a filing cabinet, waste bin etc. This allowed the Macintosh to map onto a natural system as the screen was designed to resemble the office. An immediate understanding of the object was brought about by using natural mappings. In contrast, operations on the PC frequently required a sequence of multi-key presses based on rules. In essence the Mac used our understanding of the real world, while the PC required rote memory, and there was no clear relationship between the key press and the action the computer made as a result. The success of natural mapping is evidenced by the extent to which PC operating systems have moved closer to those of the Macintosh so as now to be indistinguishable from them. The visibility of the object and parts of the object are critical in creating affordances.

Human beings respond in interesting ways when things go wrong with modern machinery. Often when a switch is thrown and nothing happens the naive operator of the video or computer assumes they have 'broken' something in the machine. We believe there should be a response to our actions. Worse occurs when we hit a key or turn a switch and something actually does go wrong. We then attribute the breakdown to have been caused by our actions. Well designed objects provide feedback that something is happening. A good example of this is the small clock icon on a computer screen in which the hands turn to indicate that something is being saved to disk, or the messages that come up to indicate what our most recent action on the machine has done. The provision of feedback limits false attributions of causality.

Natural mapping Good design incorporates all these things: visibility of functions, natural mapping to promote understanding, clues or feedback on the results of actions. In essence, the mental model that the user brings to the world needs to relate to the object to make its functions transparent. Good design uses the models that individuals have in their heads and incorporates them into the design features of the object. Unfortunately, this is not always the case in modern technology, but if the development of the computer provides a clue as to how things will develop, mapping onto natural systems will increase.

Mental models are useful as they allow us to take our knowledge and move from one object to another with some information about how the object may work. The mobile telephone incorporates the basic features of the standard telephone and provides clues to how the other features such as picking the receiver up and putting it down may work. It uses actual images of these actions even though they are not possible on the mobile, because they map onto our understanding of telephones in general. This fits with consumers' preferences: people want their mobile phones to be just like their home phones. This building of understanding is necessary to make the bridge from one technology to another. It is obviously easier when the functions are similar and more difficult when they are not. (Fax machines resemble photocopiers but perform a different function which challenges our basic understanding as the image is transmitted.)

Technologies that do not map onto natural understandings force us to rely on written information and instruction. Having information easily available in our mental models is more efficient because nothing new has to be learned to use the object. The ability to use our current understandings and apply them without learning a whole series of new operations that are not clear in the object is known as transparent functioning.

Humans can be tenacious, empirical scientists, and will not give up on a problem easily. Cause and effect is the basis of our understanding; we look for immediate feedback for our actions. When we are frustrated by a particularly daunting problem, we resort to more complex mental gymnastics. We rise to new challenges, creating new mental models of how things work and equipping ourselves to tackle similar problems in the future.

Chapter 5

Fear, Risk and Excitement

The flip side of fear is survival, and there was a charge to be had from recognizing that terror on ninth avenue at five in the morning was absolutely reasonable, and then kicking that terror in the teeth.
STEPHEN BROOK, *New York Days, New York Nights*

Anything seems possible in the modern city. Swimming pools defy gravity at the top of tall buildings.

City fears and phobias

The modern city defies nature in so many ways: it sends us up buildings dozens of storeys tall; below ground into dark winding tunnels; into metal boxes tavelling at lethal speeds. Human beings evolved to be afraid of situations like heights, tunnels and enclosed spaces because in our ancestral habitat they would have signalled a potential threat. No doubt our ancestors would find the world we take for granted literally terrifying.

The most common human fears are of heights, storms, enclosures, flying, injury, illness, and death. It is often suggested that many of these fears are linked to earlier stages in our evolution. They may be remnants of older forms of self-defensive behaviour with a rationale related to actual physical dangers that were encountered, such as fears of open spaces and attack. They may be responses to situations that in earlier times would have been so unnatural as to provoke extreme fear, such as flying.

For a fear to become a phobia it needs to cause significant distress and interference with someone's life. The number of people who have phobias reflect this. When ascertaining the number of people having phobias by asking a representative sample of the population, excessive fear of illness and injury tops the list with 31 in every 1,000 people having a fear sufficient to rate as a phobia. The box below lists the most common phobias.

Agoraphobia and claustrophobia Agoraphobia, the fear of open spaces, purports to go back to our evolutionary fear of the vulnerability to attack when in open spaces. Translated into its modern idiom, it is a fear of going outside someone's territory, usually outside the home. In its severest form, agoraphobia restricts people totally to their home or room.

In its milder form, people restrict themselves from certain areas of the city and as a result certain activities. The extent to which agoraphobia can interrupt normal life in the city can be significant: ordinary, everyday, activities such as shopping are restricted, as well as meeting other people. The ability to work outside the home becomes impossible in severe instances.

Another fear which also purports to be evolutionary in nature is that of being enclosed in small confined spaces, or claustrophobia. In the city, this means areas such as lifts or underground trains, for example. This fear allegedly goes back to the days when self defence meant ensuring you were never trapped in an enclosed

NO. OF PEOPLE IN THE POPULATION WITH AN EXTENSIVE FEAR OR PHOBIA	
	People per thousand
Illness or injury	31
Storms	13
Animals	11
Agoraphobia (fear of open spaces)	6
Death	5
Crowds	4
Heights	4

area which offered no direction of escape, literally with your back against the wall. Claustrophobia appears to be related to two different anxieties. One is about being restricted and the other being suffocated.

People who suffer from agoraphobia or claustrophobia appear to over- or underestimate some of the physical parameters of the situations they find themselves in – or indeed avoid. People with agoraphobia tend to overestimate the space and number of people and thus feel more fearful, while people with claustrophobia tend to underestimate how much space or air is available.

People curtail their activities as a result of both these anxieties. Two domains can trigger off these phobias. First, there are those which involve public, crowded or social situations such as department stores, supermarkets, restaurants, theatres, parties, and social gatherings. This set of anxieties combines an apprehension or dread of being in the open with a fear of socializing with other people. Second are enclosed spaces often associated with travelling. These include elevators, parking garages, enclosed places such as windowless rooms, subways and aeroplanes. The design of underground trains combines the possibility of being both trapped and buried. Going down gives the impression of the world closing in. Our sense of direction is also confused by short winding tunnels and identical walls.

Such areas are almost impossible to avoid in the city and it is remarkable that not many more people suffer from these fears to the extent that it interferes with their lives. This may yet again demonstrate the remarkable adaptability and resilience of human beings in their ability to deal with the seemingly unnatural environments which have been created in the city.

Fear of flying   Fear of flying is a particular handicap of *homo urbanus*. Flying is the major means of travel between urban areas, and restrictions in flying severely limit the mobility of those who need to undertake such journeys. It is not surprising that flying evokes particular fears for some people, but we still do it because it's a crucial part of modern-day living and because we love the thrill.

CLAUSTROPHOBIA

I don't like elevators, and in New York there's elevators everywhere. Every place I've been you have to get in an elevator. If there's stairs I'll take them.
I don't like that feeling. I feel like I don't get air. I feel that people are taking up my air, and I feel it'll get hot and . . . I get hot now thinking about it. It's just like . . . 'Oh, God, these people are taking my air; get away from me,' type of thing. It's like you want to shrink or run or something.

SHERRIE – New York

FEAR OF FLYING

I can fly, but as long as I pay no attention to looking out of the window. It's almost like it's unreal for something to be in the air. I feel like that's not natural.

JODIE – Los Angeles

I try not to think about it. I don't get on a plane kicking and screaming, but it's like the heart rates go and there's an anxiety level initially. You take your seat and once you're off the ground and you don't hear anything foreign – because I'm in tune to what things sound like – you glance over at the wing flaps, make sure they're working; you know the thing's mechanically sound.

RICHARD – New York

Large buildings necessitate lifts. This in turn can lead to problems: glass doors and windows can be difficult for those who are fearful of heights, the fear of being trapped is common in lifts.

The number of people who are fearful of flying depends on the way in which it is assessed, but some idea of the frequency of the fear and anxiety associated with flying can be gauged from a study conducted in Sweden. Six per cent of people in one study reported that they had never flown because of fear. One in ten people experienced immense fear throughout a flight. One in four revealed that they felt immense fear during some part of the flight, and about one in three reported fear when air turbulence was encountered. This means that nearly two-thirds of all people flying show some degree of apprehension or discomfort, but in only a small proportion is this sufficient to stop them from flying altogether.

Only a small proportion of people who have a fear of flying seek treatment, and they are usually motivated by a need to be able to fly for their work or career. A small number look for help because they would like to be more independent. When those seeking treatment are asked why they avoid flying, they do not all have the same reason. One group are rather like people with agoraphobia and avoid flying because they are afraid of having a panic attack while in flight. Another group avoid flying because they are afraid the aeroplane will crash.

Fear of heights We have learnt to live with – and sometimes to enjoy – many of the situations that would have evoked fear in our ancestors. They would have avoided heights because they represented a real risk of falling. Going to great heights above others, with a clear view of the sheer precipitous drops, is unusual for humans in evolutionary terms.

Fear of heights, known as acrophobia, is another anxiety city dwellers might be subject to, but most have successfully dealt with it. It is a statement of the adaptability of *homo urbanus* that people successfully cope with moving rapidly in elevators to great heights above the ground without any qualms. However, a small proportion of people have not been able to conquer this supposedly innate fear.

Sometimes, however, we find heights literally dizzying. In high buildings we feel drawn, as if by a magnet, to look out over the edge. This sense of perspective gives the impression of the world closing in around us. Our levels of arousal rise. Sometimes we get a sense of thrill which is pleasurable.

When I'm at the top of a tall building, I feel a slight motion. Particularly I feel like I'm pulled by gravity towards the ground. Not that I would jump, but I just feel sort of weird, and actually feel as though the building's swaying. So I never walk towards the window and I never look out and down. If I look straight across at the view then I'm all right. I start to calm down. It's not like hysterical panic, but I just feel the sensation.

SAUNDRA – London

What I'm afraid of is height, and if there's anything in the big city it's going on elevators that have that clear glass and you can see yourself going up, and if the building is real tall, I'm all the way against the door where I can't see. I will not look down. I feel as is I am going to fall. I feel like I lose control of my mind, as if I can just tip myself right over, almost like a curiosity, just to see how its going to feel, me flying, falling down. I don't think that if I'm on a tall building that the building's going to shake and make me fall. I think that if in look down I'm going to be seduced by the drop, and if I look at it I'll just go.

JODIE – Los Angeles

Before I lived in New York we used to come into the city, because my father worked in one of the World Trade Centers. And I can remember the first time that my mother took me to the top, to the observatory, I think it's in the second building. There's a glass partition that actually hangs over the edge, and the seats are on the glass, so you sit on a graded seat of metal and you're sitting over glass. You look straight down and, you know, this is the second highest building, I think, in the US at least, or maybe in the world, and it'll drop straight down. I remember my mother took me there as a child with my brother, and I was hysterical; I was just shaking.

CLIFTON – New York

We have learned to live with and enjoy things our ancestors might have feared such as great heights. Extremely tall buildings such as the World Trade Centre, are a testament not only to the ingenuity of architectural design but to the adaptability of homo urbanus.

Violence, crime and burglary

Our biggest fear in the city stems not from places that defy nature, but from places and people we do not know. Humans can have a burning desire to know the world around them, to be in control. But the city is so vast we can't know it all, and the unknown breeds the threat of crime and violence.

Violence in the city Violence to people, in particular murder, is one of the ways in which the city is sometimes characterized. While larger cities generally have higher levels of crime, the picture painted by detractors of the city as an urban wasteland full of criminals intent on murder and robbery is over simplistic. As anyone reading the news knows, some of the worst murders in recent memory have occurred in small towns, often among people known to each other. Among adults, about half of violent crimes are committed against people who the perpetrator knows. Random crimes are considerably fewer than most people imagine.

Criminal statistics are notoriously subject to error because many crimes are not reported to the police. This means most figures underestimate crime.

Within countries, there seems to be a direct relationship between the size of a city and likelihood of crimes such as drugs, burglary and robbery, but not murder. What is remarkable in relation to big-city crime is how changes in policing methods, inner city renewal (in parts of the United States) and changes in drug usage, for instance, have led to a dramatic fall in the crime rate, and in particular murder. The number of murders in New York has halved in recent years.

The murder rate in New York was considerably higher than in London until recently. New York has undergone a dramatic change in its murder rate, largely attributed to changes in policing. In 1990, there were 2,245 murders in New York City. By 1995, there were less than 1,200. This startling decline coincided with the introduction of 7,000 additional police officers into the New York Police Department and a new form of aggressive policing that no longer ignores small crimes as before. In addition, it targets the hot spots of crime. The idea behind the policy is that by paying attention to these small crimes, the culture of crime will alter and ultimately, reduce big crimes.

A number of other factors may also be important in explaining the fall of crime. One is that the pattern of drug use has altered with a reduction in the use of crack and cocaine, particularly destructive drugs. The

A successful strategy to combat fear in the city is to walk purposefully and not show any trepidation or nervousness.

percentage of young people arrested in Manhattan and found to be positive for cocaine dropped from 69 per cent to 17 per cent over the six years up to 1994. In addition there has been a considerable increase in the prison population which may have led to those most involved in crime to have been taken off the streets.

Whatever reason or reasons for the decline in crime, as a consequence tourism has increased in New York and people are reported to be walking in neighbourhoods previously considered unsafe.

Personal robbery is significantly more common in cities with populations over 250,000 than in cities with populations of less than 250,000. In these larger cities, most violent crimes of robbery are concentrated in the inner city. Three major factors may account for this. In the inner area of large cities, there is a juxtaposition of people of different socioeconomic status and more transitory visitors than residents, both of which increase the likelihood of crime by increasing first, a concentration of potential targets, the wealthy; second, a concentration of potential offenders; and finally, an absence of suitable guardians who have a stake in the inner city.

In the United States, murder is the exception to the rule that there is a higher incidence of crime

in urban areas. This is largely due to the particular characteristics of rural and traditional societies in the United States. The preponderance of guns is probably no less in rural areas than urban, and their culture of guns and machismo may match the influence of drugs and urban deprivation on crime in American inner cities.

Burglary It is a common belief that high levels of unemployment lead to higher levels of crime against property. However this view is not supported by data from Canada which shows that in 1989 in Newfoundland, with a high unemployment rate of 16 per cent, property crime was a third lower than British Columbia which had a low unemployment rate of 9 per cent. Further support for the view that it is not unemployment that encourages property crime comes from the finding that most juvenile offenders are employed at the time of their arrest.

The annual probability of a household being burgled in any one year both in North America and the United Kingdom is about one in twenty. This average figure masks a large variation which is dependent upon characteristics of the neighbourhood. Poor areas have more crime than rich ones and also attract different burglars. Rich neighbourhoods tend to attract the older, more professional burglar, while poorer neighbourhoods have younger burglars who often live in the locality. Studies have also found that neighbourhoods with lower levels of social cohesion, close proximity to major roads, and a larger proportion of mixed commercial and residential properties are more likely to suffer burglary.

Many people who commit house burglaries first evaluate a potential target much like anybody would in weighing up a course of action. As such, the nature of the property is likely to influence their behaviour. Properties least likely to be burgled in the city are those which are more densely packed together with neighbours living close by. Properties that are isolated, accessible, close to open spaces and not overlooked, are more likely to be burgled. Access is important and there is evidence that houses in cul-de-sacs are less likely to be burgled. These factors outweigh the effects of the general area when considering the likelihood of any particular property being burgled. Some properties have been found to have an annual risk rate as low as one chance in 1,500, while other properties (which have some of the high-risk characteristics mentioned) have an annual risk rate as high as a one in five chance of being burgled.

A number of studies have shown that

BURGLARY: CHARACTERISICS OF HIGH-RISK NEIGHBOURHOODS

* **more major thoroughfares**
* **more commercial and mixed land use**
* **more permeable boundaries**
* **more multi-family units**
* **more poor areas close by**
* **more public parking and vacant land**
* **less social cohesion**

BURGLARY: CHARACTERISICS OF HIGH-RISK NEIGHBOURHOODS

In general, a high degree of accessibility and more heterogeneity in land use leads to more strangers being present and unnoticed by residents in the area.

areas with certain characteristics have a higher propensity to burglary. These include edges of areas, heterogeneous areas, areas of high activity, and areas that are run down; and there are usually good reasons why they have a higher chance of burglary. It is often apparent when crossing the border from one area to another, particularly when the border is marked, as it often is, by a park or a main road. These borders or edges, the transition from one area to another, are subject to higher levels of crime. Similarly, moving into a heterogeneous neighbourhood where there are different types of buildings such as houses, small businesses, and garages, more crimes tend to be committed.

The high level of burglary apparent at edges and heterogeneous areas may be due to the larger number of strangers there and the fact that residents are less likely to notice a potential burglar as anything unusual. When two different types of area are close to each other, it is also likely that people are more accepting of the presence of strangers as they assume they have come from the other area. This is the reverse of the phenomenon of the cul-de-sac where strangers would be noticed. Some criminologists suggest that criminal activity is lowest where the design of an area makes it more private, supervisable, and where residents recognize each other – characterized as defensible space. To some extent, this underestimates the possibility of the criminal being an 'insider' to the area.

Most cities have particular sites or hot spots where a large proportion of all crimes are committed. For example, in a two-block radius in Vancouver, Canada, one-sixth of all homicides occurred over a seven-year period. Data demonstrates that a similar pattern occurs for other less serious crimes in most cities. It seems that people intent on crimes often travel to a particular area. Where they go appears to relate to the likelihood of potential victims, surveillance, and of being caught.

Crimes also tend to occur when the area is known to the burglar. A reasonably high proportion of burglary is committed by insiders who have an intimate knowledge of the locality, apartment block or building. In some cases, these crimes are opportunistic. In general, more crimes occur in areas or at times when there is a lot of activity such as shopping centres, train stations, or pub-closing times, and where many people pass by. It is important that burglars have mental maps of cities and these influence their understanding of the possibility of movement from a crime. The result is that burglary tends to occur around areas of high activity, close to major transport nodes (such as a bus station) and near highways. Not only do these factors make properties accessible, but they also come into the mental map of the burglar: that is, he has a knowledge of the area.

Signs of care in an area such as newly painted doors, neatness, and the absence of garbage and vandalism give the appearance that there is someone who cares and, therefore, watches over an area. This reduces the attractiveness of an area for a burglar as they feel they may be seen and noticed.

Burglaries in city areas, where there are high-rise apartments, also show a particular pattern. Not surprisingly, ground-floor apartments have the highest burglary rates. Second-floor apartments are next, followed by top- floor apartments. Mid-level apartments have the lowest burglary rates with the result that overall comparisons between high- and low-rise apartments in any area show that high-rise apartments as a whole have a low level of burglary.

For many people, shoplifting from a large store is a crime without a clear victim. But in some countries, the development of shopping malls as places where people can congregate, meet others, socialize, and relax watching others, has led to the malls becoming major areas of crime. In the main, this involves shoplifting, but as shopping malls are now high-activity areas, other criminal activity – such as pick-pocketing, bag-snatching and mugging – has followed.

Fear is a very personal thing. Every city dweller experiences different levels of fear in different places, but in general, as we move away from familiar territory, our perception of control decreases and our sense of vulnerability and unease starts to increase.

Judging danger City dwellers often miscalculate what is dangerous. The dark may reduce our sense of control, but much crime actually takes place in the city in daylight hours. There are no statistics to prove we are

People feel more anxious about being attacked in dark places. Meeting a single stranger in an isolated and graffiti strewn area tends to be judged as risky.

My chances of being attacked? Seventy per cent. There's been some near misses sometimes.

ALEX – London

I think the chances are probably 50 per cent. It's so random, so thoughtless, they're really quick these days to shoot you.

VERONICA – Los Angeles

The lifestyle I lead and the places I go, I would say about, there's about 20 per cent chance that I could be attacked.

PINKY – London

Well, I heard some statistic, like in LA one out of every four women are supposed to be the victim of rape.

KATH – Los Angeles

more vulnerable in litter-strewn streets than in clean ones. In fact, although violent crime is more prevalent in the city than outside it, most of us still wildly overestimate our chances of being victims.

When analysing people's reactions to crime, a distinction must be made between the direct experience when an individual was the object of a crime, and the indirect experience of knowing or hearing about a crime.

There is an extremely important general finding that the fear of crime and the direct experience of crime are not related. In some studies, people who were more frightened of crime often had a lower risk of being the victim of crime. The British Social Attitudes Survey in 1995, however, showed that although a general fear of crime was not related to being a victim, those people who had direct experience of crime were more likely to alter their behaviour because of their relative fear.

Vicarious experience of crime Hearing about criminal episodes from friends, neighbours, or through the local media has a dramatic effect on people's fear of crime. The more people hear about crimes having been committed in their neighbourhood the more afraid they become. The more similar the victim is perceived to be to themselves, the greater the impact of hearing about the crime.

Ironically, in more socially cohesive neighbourhoods, a factor which reduces the chance of crime, individuals are more likely to hear about crimes from the neighbours and friends because social contact is more frequent. The more violent the crime the more likely it is to be talked and gossiped about and the more likely it is to be picked up and reported by the media. The net effect of this is that individuals in the communities with higher social cohesion and less risk of crime have higher levels of fear.

Studies particularly about crime to the person have found this to be so. A large number of people are frightened about this kind of crime despite the fact that, statistically, they are extremely unlikely to experience it. Although these fears might be irrational, nonetheless policy makers often consider strategies to reduce the fear of crime, rather than crime itself. An example of this is more visible policing: in London, more bobbies (police) on the beat.

Certain crimes gain a notoriety because of their novelty. Notable among these is carjacking. Not only does carjacking pierce the wall of protection that we believe the car offers but it also has a reputation of being accompanied with random violence. It is a crime of recent years, picked up and developed by the media, and is often reported as a fear in some cities. Many drivers in areas reputed to suffer from carjacking are more alert when they drive. In particular, they tend to be more aware of locking doors, but they also take avoiding action by trying to keep moving, anticipating red traffic lights and being aware of others around them.

A recent review of research on the fear of crime suggests that people's fear is less to do specifically with becoming a victim, than a general feeling of insecurity with the modern world. The British Social Attitudes Survey of 1995 found a link between some people's fear of crime and the extent to which they worried about life in general. This was less clear cut among women and younger men than among older men. Attitudes towards crime seem to be combined with other general social attitudes.

REACTIONS TO ROBBERY

I heard her babbling on a couple of feet behind me: 'Why don't you rob somebody with money!' and that sort of thing, and one guy was yelling to the other guy, Come on, let's go, let's go, let's go!' And they finally took off. It was interesting at the time, I wasn't scared at all, and then for about two or three weeks I was constantly looking over my shoulders thinking I was going to be attacked. I had fantasies that these two guys were going to come back and get me and that sort of thing.

JOHN – New York

FEAR OF CARJACKING

It's kinda scary because there's nobody out there and you're like the only car and who knows what can happen – carjacking. And its just not cool to be in the wrong neighbourhood at the wrong time. You hear about people getting shot or robbed or worse.

SCOTT – Los Angeles

If you go there and you see a lot of people on the streets, let's turn away and lock your car doors or roll up your windows because you don't know what they're going to do. And that's anybody; you don't know if they're going to jack you for your car or try to sell drugs to you. You have to stay aware, stay alert.

DANIEL – Los Angeles

I'm always cognisant of where I am and who's behind me and who's on the side of me, just for my own protection. Of course, you see so much on TV that you know these things are happening, even though they're not happening to you. So they're frightening. Every minute on TV there's something going on that's bad.

RONNIE – Los Angeles

If it's a minicab (unregistered taxi) then you don't know who the person is: they're just working for a minicab firm, so I get him to drop me off either outside my house and I walk past and then walk back after they've gone, or drop me off somewhere down the road so that they don't actually know where I live. I sometimes go to somebody else's front door and sort of fiddle about at the door a bit and then when they've gone, come back out again.

CLARE – London

I think that sometimes you can get to the point where you will stop doing things as a fear of that. So . . . I do take certain precautions. I become quite conscious, I lock the doors in the car when I'm driving; I'll park in lighted areas.

PINKY – London

It's really scary in Los Angeles because its a gang thing. . . . I've walked out of my house and seen somebody just pop another guy off in broad daylight with about twenty witnesses all around. When I'm walking I just have a realization that every kid you see is packing a gun because that's just the way it is in society today in America – it's almost as if we're living in the wild west.
I live with a pit bull who sleeps in bed with me at night and I wouldn't feel safe if he wasn't in my bed. I would feel absolutely terrified to go to sleep at night if I didn't have this kind of security.

KENYA – Los Angeles

At two-thirty in the morning you've got the possible people breaking people's windows and their cars and suspicious characters. There's no one around actually to help you. Once you've gone past the security guard of the building you're in, there's nobody who would actually notice anything going on on the streets of London. And then I was scared. A couple of times, I've had my umbrella ready, just in case,

SAUNDRA – London

Aspects of fear

Gender Surveys show women are more frightened of crime than men, although it is possible that some men find it difficult to acknowledge their fear when responding to questions about crime and assault. The difference between the genders is not surprising and is largely attributed to the fear of sexual assault.

Age Older people tend to be more fearful than younger people when asked about being in public areas, such as walking home at night. At older age levels the differences between men and women decline, with older men being as fearful as older women. This is interesting as it is in the opposite direction to objective risk which declines with age for men. When asked about fear in their homes, age does not seem to have an effect on fear. It is clear that older people are more fearful than younger people in public spaces at night, and not when in their territory. Increasing age and fear of crime is particularly prevalent among city residents with rural origins.

Rural origins It is often thought that people who come to a city from a rural or small town environment bring with them naive views and fears of big city life. The size of the town that people come from has a substantial effect on their fear of crime. Those people coming from smaller towns tend to be more fearful of crime that people coming from larger towns. This effect is, however, short-lived as new arrivals begin to accommodate to the city and become less fearful. Among people who had been in the city less than two years, the larger the community of origin, the safer they felt in the city. This link did not apply among longer-term residents who had lived in the city for over two years. The lower level of fear felt by people coming from larger communities suggests they have a more realistic perspective about the general nature of the city. Nonetheless, even those from smaller towns adapt fairly quickly, losing much of their fear within two years. As with friendships, the process of acculturation into the city does not take long.

Risky places People tend to form a mental template of an area which is likely to be potentially dangerous. They use these templates or models when negotiating around a city and become more on their guard when an area or situation fits more closely with it. Although these templates differ between individuals there are some general features of an environment which most people would judge to be risky.

A decline in the visible social fabric of an area is an important one:

when areas show signs of decay, such as unoccupied and unmaintained houses, vandalism, graffiti, vagrants in the streets, or uncollected garbage, the fear of crime increases. These indicators of the state of an area are associated in people's minds with a belief that there has been a breakdown in social order and results in a fear of the unpredictability to which that breakdown leads. The factor found to be most associated with fear of crime in this respect is vandalism.

People living in areas which were previously stable but now show signs of decay are more likely to have raised fears about crime than people living in areas which have not changed. Areas that are maintained in good order seem to protect people from feelings of fear about crime. Even individuals who have been the victims of crime are less likely to be fearful of it if they live in well maintained neighbourhoods, than victims living in areas that show signs of disorder and decay.

High-rise buildings have also been associated with higher crime. Interestingly, when elderly tenants were asked about fear of crime, they were less afraid than tenants in low-rise buildings. Their judgements were unrelated to the incidence if actual crime.

Having lots of people around tends to make individuals feel safe. However, data suggests that a counteracting force may be at work in some situations. People may feel more afraid when they are in the presence of strangers. For instance, some studies show that people living in large buildings where they have less control of the external space and where strangers often use the public areas feel more insecure. In fact, our fear appears to be of other people, in particular of people we don't know and with whom we have not chosen to interact.

Lighting Outdoor public areas are important in the city and the fear of crime in these areas is particularly related to two factors: the number of people around and about, and the time of day. When two or more people are present in a public environment, it tends to be rated as more desirable than one that is deserted. People also tend to prefer public places at dawn rather than dusk, presumably because dusk is followed by night when people would feel less safe, and dawn by day when more people would be around. In general, when people are asked about those areas of a city in which they feel most unsafe they refer to areas that are deserted, poorly lit, and quiet. These fears bear little relationship to the actual levels of crime in an area.

Lighting has been used as a crime reduction technique in cities for many years. London and Paris introduced lighting as long ago as the

People form a mental template of potentially dangerous areas and are therefore rapidly able to make an assessment of danger on the streets.

People feel safer when two or more other people are present in public spaces as long as they are all together in a group.

Areas of the city which show signs of decay such as graffiti, especially dark, poorly lit places provoke fear.

eighteenth century to reduce crime on the streets at night. The function of lighting is both to allow people to see others approaching them, and also to enable someone who needs help to be visible.

The introduction of lighting into an area that was previously unlit has been found to have a significant effect on crime. But lighting changes must be substantial and perceptible to be effective. Small changes in lighting in some studies have shown few effects on actual crime. It is interesting that improvements in lighting alter people's feelings about crime in an area. In one important study, researchers assessed the levels of fear of crime in an area before, and after, improved levels of lighting were introduced. When the lighting improved, people generally felt safer on the streets and felt that they would receive help faster than they did when the area was poorly lit.

Lighting has been used as a method of reducing crime for many years, but it must be used at a substantial level to have any effect.

Green spaces

Parks have now become one of the most valuable parts of the urban landscape. In addition to ecological concerns, introducing parks and vegetation into an urban environment has a number of other effects. One suggestion is that trees make a city appear smaller and therefore easier to comprehend. Another is that parks and green spaces in a city offer unregulated and wild spaces in an otherwise controlled and managed world.

The view that trees make a city seem safer is questionable; for many people, trees are simply a means of obscuring the view. Nonetheless, studies of urban environments do suggest that when vegetation is introduced, individuals rate the area more positively and feel that it offers a better quality of life, as well as being safer. In addition, individuals rate areas as more pleasurable when trees are added. It is not that the area with trees is seen as less urban, but its quality as an urban area is judged to have improved.

Although people prefer having parks in their cities and neighbourhoods, these green spaces can also have problems of their own. Certainly, parks play an important social role in the city, but issues of security and safety are increasingly coming on to the agenda.

In daylight hours, parks are attractive, open spaces, often quieter than their surrounds. At night, however, parks and trees can be dangerous areas which are best avoided until it is light again. Time of day, therefore, has a major effect on the perception of parks. In adapting to this, some park keepers are introducing floodlights, others more social events, both to encourage people to use parks and prevent them becoming isolated, dangerous public spaces.

People who live in cities seek out parks, at least during daylight hours, and have expectations that these green spaces will produce the warm, comforting emotions they do not get in other urban and suburban areas of the city. How the park is designed, and in particular, how many trees it has will influence how much pleasure they get from walking in the park.

But making cities more green can only have a limited impact, for those of us who are in cities live in a busy and crowded world.

FEAR OF PARKS AT NIGHT

I don't really like to be out at night unless I'm with somebody. If I drive home and I have to park and it's dark, I get panicky, because I have to walk from the car to the stairs and there are trees all around, and I always think there is somebody standing there.

ESTHER – Los Angeles

CCTV

In the face of reductions in funding for police personnel, city authorities are beginning to rely on technology to provide a presence in the inner city. Surveillance or potential surveillance is known to be a major deterrent of crime because it increases the perceived and actual risks of criminals being caught. It is known that wider and less visible streets have higher levels of crime.

It is, therefore, not surprising that the use of close circuit television (CCTV) cameras has increased dramatically in city centres, buildings, and major transport locations such as train and bus stations. While the deterrent value of this is important, the increased use and publicity of CCTV in city centres also provides the policing authorities with the ability to respond quickly to crimes. CCTV goes some way to reassure the public that help is always close at hand. Most importantly, CCTV leads to an increase in conviction rates. In general, where there are cameras, there is a decline in some types of crime; in particular that of car theft and burglary.

However, there is some concern that the effect of CCTV is to transfer the activity out of the range of the cameras and thus it acts only to displace crime.

IMPACT OF FEAR OF VIOLENCE

You've got to really watch out for how you speak to people and who you piss off, because you never know what could happen. [I try] to be more in control emotionally, not to fly off the handle with people that I don't know, that are strangers, because if you do that you're taking your life into your hands. It's kind of like a risk, it's just a big risk and really scary.

You have to be really careful about driving in this city because apparently it's appropriate for everybody to have their own piece of firearm equipment. So if you flip somebody off in your car or call somebody a jerk or whatever – and I'm being most polite right now – you are taking a great chance of getting shot in the head. Basically, there isn't a day that goes by that you don't turn on the news and hear about somebody on the freeway getting shot by another driver.

KENYA – Los Angeles

Everyone feels afraid at certain times. It just depends on the situation. I'm not afraid to walk the streets here. There's certain areas where you just know you'd better not go at night by yourself and hang out. You try to avoid those areas.

DAVE – Los Angeles

My biggest fear about living in the city is being attacked. I'm a single girl and I live alone so I pay much more rent than I would like to so that I can be in a safe neighbourhood, in a safe, secured building. I always try and be observant of my surroundings if I have to go some place at night where I have to park, I always try and find a street lamp to park directly under. I always try and check the back seat of the car before I get into it. I'll sort of glance under to make sure there's no one hiding under it. I walk briskly . . .

VERONICA – Los Angeles

Coping with fear

Limiting what we do   Fear of crime is a social problem because it limits the amount of social interaction that occurs. People who are most fearful of crime in public areas are less likely to venture out and meet others. An analysis of National Crime Survey data for 6,500 respondents in 26 cities in the USA suggests that fear and constrained social behaviour are part of a spiral where fear of crime restricts social interaction which in turn increases fear. The older people are, the more likely this is to happen.

The British Social Attitudes survey indicated in 1995 that a third of women and a quarter of men think that fear of crime alters how they behave. As well as ensuring that they lock up their houses and cars, the most important ways in which people alter their behaviour is avoiding going to certain places (44 per cent of women and 35 per cent of men), going out at certain times only (43 per cent of women and 15 per cent of men) and ensuring that other family members take precautions (40 per cent women and 44 per cent men). In addition, nearly one in six women do not go out alone.

The fear of crime has an impact on families with young children. In New York, parents are found to believe that certain places are particularly dangerous for their children. Ironically, these are the very places established for children's enjoyment, such as parks and playgrounds. But, because parents are afraid of the social dangers to their children in these particular urban environments, they tend to restrict the play activity of their children there.

In London, most parents do not rate their neighbourhoods as safe. A recent survey showed that only one out of fifty parents rated their neighbourhoods as secure for their children. Only about one in seven parents would let their ten-year-old child walk to school unaccompanied. The interesting point is that the large majority of parents who restrict their children in this way were not restricted themselves when they were the same age: nearly 70 per cent walked to school at the age of ten. These restrictions on children are thought to have increased because the fear of violence to children has grown.

A lot of the fear for children revolves around a fear of what strangers may do. While there is a common belief that the incidence of murder of small children has increased considerably in recent years, it is not supported by the evidence. Between 1983 and 1993 in England and Wales, the average number of children under the age of sixteen years who were murdered every year was eighty-six, and this did not change. Again, contrary to common belief, this was not done by strangers, but the vast majority were murdered by parents or guardians.

The emotional effects of the fear of crime are apparent on parents and children. Parents' fears about social threats to their children show up in their own tensions and anxieties. For children, constant information about the possibility of social danger in public places tends to make them more frightened.

Fear of crime has an impact on the maps people use to navigate around the city. Women actively avoid areas they know to be dangerous, while men avoid areas with which they are unfamiliar. The idea of being 'street wise' or having 'street savvy' is an important part of being able to avoid crime on the street. This makes *homo urbanus* receptive to learning the safe areas in a city when moving to new locations, unlike a country dweller who may either see the city as a place to be fearful of wherever he or she is, or alternatively be naive to the idea of safe areas.

Hiding fear Besides altering where they go, people also alter how they behave. Being sensitive to others and not behaving in a way that will increase the likelihood of becoming a victim of attack are common strategies. Common amongst these behaviours is to appear purposeful and not to show any fear when moving about in areas of the city which feel threatening.

For most city dwellers, the fear of violence has altered their behaviour by restricting it. This may be a testament to our adaptive skills, but it creates a vicious circle too. Fear drives us into the protection of our homes, so the streets become emptier. And emptier streets create more fear. By shutting ourselves away from the city, we have not reduced our fear of violence, instead we have increased it.

Sometimes I've acted as if I'm a bit mad, because you don't tend to approach people if they look a bit loopy, so I talk to myself or something, or whistle or sing. I just act a bit loopy and people might think I'm strange and leave me alone.

CLARE – London

I finish work late, so then I have to get from the station to home. The area's well lit but you're still aware of everyone who's around you. And if somebody is behind you then you glance round. If it's a man or a woman who's coming towards you, you make yourself a bit bigger and puff your shoulders up and clench your fist as well to say you're ready or something.

JANE – London

I walk down the street with that attitude. I don't look like this kind of lost little wallflower anywhere. I look like I have a place to be and I'm going there. And if you want to take me on, I'm up for it.

KENYA – Los Angeles

I find that you can't look like you're afraid, and you can't look like you don't know where you're going, because if it is a tough neighbourhood, and there is a situation that is very possible and probable to happen then you would probably attract more attention to yourself in that manner. One of the rules is if you're in a situation like that, you look people in the eye, let them see that you're looking at them.

PEPSI – New York

One thing about New York is that you're always told never to look anybody straight in the eyes because you don't want to provoke somebody. I tend to wear sunglasses on the subway because I can make eye contact, I can look at somebody, I can observe them without them seeing me, and it's kind of this incognito costume I wear.

CLIFTON – New York

Risk taking and seeking thrills

Fear and excitement We may feel a growing fear of attack, but overall our world is safer than it has ever been before. Humans dislike too much safety as much as too much fear. When we feel safe, we often look for ways to make the world exciting.

Excitement and fear are two sides of the same coin. Physiologically, our responses are almost identical. What differs is our psychological interpretation of these repsonses. What makes us excited rather than afraid is a sense that we have taken this risk voluntarily.

Arousal The physiological states in arousal entail the activity of the autonomic nervous system (that is the part which is not under our control). Breathing quickens to take more oxygen into the body; the heart beats faster, carrying more blood along with oxygen and sugar to the muscles and the brain; respiration is faster, taking more oxygen into the body to travel with the blood; the brain becomes more aroused and we feel more alert and ready for quick action. The physiological response cannot determine whether we define arousal as excitement or anxiety. This is a matter upon which we make a judgement. The critical difference between the two is that one state of arousal is perceived to be pleasurable, while the other is unpleasant.

Some situations are clear. For most people, awaiting the results of a medical test for a fatal illness is an anxious situation and few would see it as exciting. By contrast, watching a gripping film is exciting for most people and few would call that anxiety provoking. In both situations, however, the physiological reactions people have are essentially similar.

The reverse side of the coin are times of low arousal. These too can be defined positively or negatively, as boredom or relaxation. The physiological response is the same, but the emotion experienced differs. What emotion we attach to our experience and whether we see it as pleasurable or not is dependent upon how we interpret the situation outside our body.

We can move through these four emotions, excitement and relaxation (both pleasant), and anxiety and boredom (both unpleasant), very quickly in a fast-changing environment. We can be sipping a drink in a sidewalk cafe feeling 'pleasurably relaxed' when suddenly a lot of noise, shouting and a gunshot brings on a swift feeling of rather 'uncomfortable anxiety'. From the safety of our seat inside the cafe, we can see two people running down the street being chased by a group of policemen who apprehend them giving us a sense of 'relieved excitement'. Police cars arrive to take the two felons away and as witnesses, we are asked to wait and talk to the police. We are fifth in line to give our information and the first two individuals take some time to give their evidence moving us into our fourth sensation of 'disagreeable boredom'. In contrast to the placid countryside, our level of arousal is raised at all times in the busy, noisy city, and we can move rapidly between these emotions.

Taking risks We normally associate fear and excitement with physical activities such as fast driving, skiing and motor racing. These activities can make us feel we are actually flirting with death and that may be the ulti- mate fear and thrill. People doing these things report a rush of excitement coupled with a clarity of attention not experienced at any other time.

But not all times of excitement and fear are so dramatic as ones involv- ing physical risk. There is a wide range of other activities that are exciting

We regularly flirt with danger in the city. The most common form of risk taking in the city is crossing a road within a few feet of large masses of moving steel which can kill in an instant.

and at times frightening. Traditional gambling as well as speculating on the stock exchange and risking financial security can be just as exciting. Scientists who put their reputations on the line when following an important scientific discovery can risk their self esteem and prestige for a sense of excitement. There are many other non-physical but risky situations which may induce excitement or fear such as giving an important speech, or changing jobs.

As the quotation at the start of this chapter indicates, for some people the excitement of being at risk also provides enormous rewards which make the risk-taking behaviour worthwhile. Some of the behaviour discussed above which causes fear in the city is in fact exciting for the perpetrators. For example, stealing a car to go joy riding is an exciting activity, precisely because it is tinged with danger. Some joy riders try to provoke a car chase and taunt the police by driving in front of them to get a chase going. Arousal coupled with danger is necessary in this situation to induce excitement. Similarly, people who shoplift and rob also report high levels of excitement that sometimes oscillate with fear.

The most common form of acceptable risk in the city involves proximity. When city dwellers are pedestrians they often pass within a couple of feet of huge, speeding masses of steel that could kill in an instant. Pedestrians do this all the time without feeling any particular anxiety, although they recognize the margin of safety that needs to be maintained between themselves and motor vehicles. In part, we don't feel anxious because we are used to cars and expect them to obey the rules of the road. Some pedestrians take risks by slipping in and out of traffic. For some city dwellers, these risks are taken in the rush of city life without realizing the dangers. Others like to flirt with the danger by playing a game with fast approaching traffic.

What people fear: traffic accidents

As mentioned in an earlier chapter, deaths from traffic accidents are high in most countries. The proportion of deaths occurring in urban areas tends to be smaller than those occurring on more open rural roads, largely due to speed which is an incriminating factor in many accidents. The other common incriminating factor associated with accidents and deaths is drunken driving. The majority of deaths occur among drivers and passengers but in urban areas, pedestrians are particularly at risk.

Negotiating a vehicle around the streets of a city is a highly complex activity, and one we have become very good at. It often involves making fine judgements about approaching vehicles. The major difficulty is judging the arrival time of another vehicle at an intersection. These calculations are subject to some systematic biases. For instance, judgements are influenced by the size of the other vehicle. Judgements about large vehicles such as trucks tend to be more accurate than those of small vehicles like cars. In turn, car judgements are more accurate than judgements about the arrival time of motorcycles, and so on.

This is especially important in the urban environment with its proliferation of small vehicles such as bicycles and motorbikes. It makes the urban environment more hazardous for accidents because it is more subject to possible errors regarding the judgement of arrival times. There also appear to be gender differences in judgements of arrival times. Women are more cautious in their judgements than men, and thus give themselves a greater margin of error when crossing at an intersection.

Pedestrians are at risk in the city. They tend to walk close to motor vehicles where a small movement may lead to injury. These risks are all part of moving around a busy city but emphasize the need to rapidly process information when moving about. Pedestrians are particularly at risk when they avoid using the areas specifically designed for them to cross the road, and where cars are expected to stop on a signal.

Many of the acceptable risk behaviours that we do in the city are associated with close proximity to moving solid objects such as cars or trains. Standing close to the platform when the underground train arrives is another acceptable 'risk' we take. Some newcomers may find this behaviour anxiety provoking. Others may find it exciting. For many city dwellers the behaviour is performed so often that it has become unremarkable. The effect of experience on excitement and anxiety is important in everyday behaviour and it is the unusual occurrence that leads to an increase in arousal.

An important distinction should be made between actual risk and vicarious risk, such as that which results from watching a film or seeing other people do dangerous things. For many people in the city, the modern world of information technology brings our vicarious excitement to us. We can watch thrillers in the comfort of our homes and feel the excitement and fear without taking any risk at all. The process we engage in is to put ourselves into the position of the protagonist and by being engrossed in the film, we are transported into experiencing the emotions of the individuals portrayed. A further distinction is between voluntary and involuntary risk. Various sporting activities fall into this category. A common, modern, discretionary risk is bungee jumping which has grown enormously in recent years. It is estimated that about 1,000 jumps take place in a week in the United States. What is important is that people choosing to engage in this form of risk behaviour usually do so because of the danger. To some extent, however, the danger is under their control. While there may be attendant risks, they are only a small component and the thrill dominates.

On the other hand, when danger is not sought but arises because of force of circumstances, such as having to walk home through a dark and deserted crime-ridden street in the early hours of the morning, then the danger is non-discretionary and an unwelcome threat. Generally, these sorts of threatening situations provoke anxiety. They may also be judged as exciting but not often at the time; rather afterwards when we relate the experience to others.

Regardless of whether we get our excitement vicariously or actually, whether it is involuntary or we choose it, all humans need some degree of excitement. In the city, *homo urbanus* gets his fair share.

The danger of cars It is ironic how, in the industrialized world, we feel safe and protected in an instrument that kills enormous numbers of people every year. As long ago as 1951, 1 million Americans had died on the roads. The USA still tops the list with over 40,000 people dying on the roads per year. Japan and Germany have a little over 10,000 road deaths per annum and France about 9,000. In Britain about 4,000 people die on the roads every year. This goes some way to putting our ideas of the car and security in perspective.

One of the most important factors influencing the extent of injury is the speed of the vehicle at the time of impact. This is particularly important in pedestrian accidents, 95 per cent of which occur in urban areas. In

I love the feeling of driving fast with my window open, even when it's cold, and my music on, you know. It's just about relaxing, being in control.

PINKY – London

My first car, I took it out on the freeway, through downhill roads and got up to 135 and the cop pulled me over. It's the adrenaline rush. Just like when I play video games. I mean, I want to go fast. It's how fast you can get some place. I'm one of those people that if I can go ahead of somebody in the line – that even to save fifty seconds [would do it]. If a person's going so slow I got to go around them, I can't wait for them.

DAVE – Los Angeles

Sometimes if they're going too slow I will speed up real close and cut in front of them to show them they were going too slow. I don't worry about the risks because I get a thrill out of it. I really like going fast. Actually I like the risk. If I wasn't able to do that I wouldn't have an outlet for all the energy that I have.

VERONICA – Los Angeles

I do drive quite fast, yeah. I don't think I'm putting anybody in danger. I mean if I do drive fast the road is clear. I don't accelerate at red traffic lights or a zebra (pedestrian) crossing. If there's a nice bit of road, yeah, why not, I put my foot down. I have been fined for speeding before. But I don't think I've put anybody in danger except for myself, really . . . It's a nice bit of adrenaline.

KHALID – London

I love anything to do with speed. I love speed. Everybody thinks that speed is about sort of proving this kind of macho thing. But in actuality I think that speed is about rushing into the world. It's just about embracing the world and like kissing it. It's really a wonderful thing, and I'm not afraid of it.

RICHARD – New York

collisions between motor vehicles and pedestrians, the pedestrian's chance of being killed rises dramatically with an increase in the speed of the motor vehicle. This is clearly crucial in urban areas with speed limits currently set (in the UK) at about 50 to 65km (30 to 40 miles) per hour. A reduction in motor traffic speed to approximately 30km (20 miles) per hour would not only reduce the levels of pedestrian injuries sustained in collisions, but also give both parties a better chance of avoiding the collision in the first place.

Traffic calming schemes have been introduced to force vehicles to slow down and hence decrease the danger of traffic in cities, especially in residential areas. The term 'calming', like road rage, implies that traffic is angry. Where these schemes have been tested and their effects assessed, such as in Denmark, results show that vehicle speeds are reduced significantly. Feelings of security as well as traffic safety increase. The town environments are improved and the towns become more attractive from the citizens' point of view.

A more extreme example of dealing with cars is to ban all but essential transport from city centres. The most important measure that needs to be introduced when restricting car access to city centres is the provision of cheap, regular and attractive public transport services. Some smaller European cities have introduced this policy to make their centres less noisy and polluted.

Cars and driving fast Taking risks by driving fast is generally a thrilling experience because we are taking the risks voluntarily and we have a protective framework around us. This framework is largely psychological – it's a sense that we are in control. Cars are also a symbol of power. They allow us to take control of a powerful and dangerous machine. Driving at speed and fast acceleration are considered by many to be one of the joys of owning a car. Although we are all very confident of our ability to handle a car at speed it has been claimed that 90 per cent of road crashes are due to driver error, and speed has been associated with many accidents.

When a random group of drivers in the United States were assessed, 14 per cent reported having been involved in an accident in the previous year. More importantly, a high proportion were found to take risks when driving. Eight per cent reported driving when they had too much to drink, one in five had gone through at least one red traffic light in the previous month, and nearly half said they often drove faster than the speed limit.

The driving style of younger people is more risky than that of older people. They tend to drive faster, leave less space between cars when pulling into traffic, go through amber lights, and drive closer to the car in front of them. Men, and in particular, young men do these things more often than women and older men. Not surprisingly, therefore, young men are more often implicated in traffic accidents. Women are 30 per cent less likely to have crashes than men.

Personality and risk Six dimensions of personality have been found to be related to high risk driving behaviour. These include thrill seeking, impulsiveness, hostility or anger, emotional instability, depression, and the locus of perceived control. High levels of these characteristics predispose individuals to high-risk driving or to react in such a way that they will be at a higher risk of being involved in a crash. These characteristics together account for 10 to 20 per cent of the components of traffic accidents and over a third of those associated with risky driving. In another study, when the personalities of drivers convicted for speeding or reckless driving were examined, they were found to be high in a desire for thrill seeking and also to be easily bored.

The use of the car as mechanism for seeking thrills and getting excitement is widely used in cities partly because of the easy availability of cars, the excitement and risks of speed, and the importance of the car in urban life.

Power games When vehicles and pedestrians come into contact, the regulation of behaviour becomes important, partly because of the potential of the car to inflict lethal damage. In most cities, rules govern the relationship between walker and driver. These rules differ. Some favour the pedestrian, as in many American cities where, if the pedestrian wishes to cross the road, cars must come to a halt. In England a more limited system favouring pedestrians is used: pedestrians have specific crossing paths marked by a flashing beacon where they have right of way over cars and other vehicles. In other cities the system is more directly tied to the rules governing the flow of cars: pedestrians may cross roads when cars are stopped to allow the opposing flow to progress. In some cities, the rules governing pedestrians are less apparent and crossing roads requires much greater skill.

Some situations require active give and take between drivers and walkers. Pedestrians can decide when it is convenient to cross for the cars, and car drivers can be more or less responsive to a pedestrian's desire to cross the road. Studies have compared the tendency of older and younger motorists to stop for a pedestrian wishing to cross the road. Interestingly, the researchers initially proposed that older drivers would be more likely to go through a crossing and not respond to pedestrians because of their reduced capacity for attention. In other words, they believed stopping behaviour would be governed by driving skill and the cognitive abilities of drivers. The results revealed the opposite. Younger drivers are less likely than older drivers to stop for someone obviously approaching to cross the road. This suggests that the behaviour of car drivers in responding to pedestrians has little to do with the driver's ability and is more likely to be something under their own control and subject to each driver's choice.

Even in cities with some regulation over pedestrians and cars there are marginal situations where each vies for control. Classic amongst these is a situation of 'pedestrian resistance' against cars, where the pedestrian crosses against the light to force the car to stop. In another form, the pedestrian walks directly across the road, forcing cars to stop. The driver of the car is given a simple choice by the pedestrian: either give way and let me pass or run me down. Pedestrian resistance to the supremacy of the car is very common in cities because most road regulations are designed to increase the flow of cars. Only recently have more attempts been made to restrict the role of the car in favour of those who are walking.

Pedestrians also engage in a milder form of pedestrian resistance. Once their fight with the car driver has been won, they assert their dominance, by walking slowly across the road.

The behaviour of car drivers is more responsive to the needs of disabled pedestrians. Attitudes to disability in Western societies are often a

PEDESTRIAN RESISTANCE

I have had a situation when I was crossing and these cab drivers they try to ride up as close to you as they can, just to let you know: 'Hey, buddy . . . I'll take you out of here! This is New York, you don't step off the kerb when it's time for me to go! You'd better be on the kerb.' Yes, I will challenge these guys and walk out on the street because I'm thinking, 'Jeez, if he hits me, I can win a million dollars and then retire for life,' or something like that.

GERALD – New York

'Pedestrian resistance' to the car's supremacy on the road is common in the city.

Drivers and pedestrians often engage in a battle of wills for dominance of the road.

complex mix of concern and disparagement towards the disabled person. To some extent these are reflected in the behaviour of car drivers. Research indicates that drivers are much more likely to give way to a disabled pedestrian with a white cane indicating partial sight or blindness, than to an able-bodied person attempting to cross a pedestrian crossing.

Negotiating complex intersections can create particular problems for certain pedestrians such as older citizens. Studies in a German town, of situations in which accidents occurred, showed that elderly people are especially at risk. The main problems are related to the speed and variability of the traffic as well as the complexity of streets and traffic intersections for the elderly. Situations of complexity often cause stress and anxiety among older people which in turn may lead unwittingly to hazardous behaviour on their part.

Forcing the car to stop is a victory for the pedestrian.

The group most at risk from accidents between pedestrians and cars are children. The risk of pedestrian injury to children under fifteen years is higher than that of all other age groups when adjusted for traffic exposure. Children appear to react on the spur of the moment and rush across roads without taking into account the risks. In addition, they tend to cross at places where cars and pedestrian interaction is unregulated. Consequently, the most frequently observed accident type is when children dart out to the middle of a road from between parked cars.

We have grown so accustomed to the dangers of the city that most of them pass us by. We enjoy risk, treading as close as we dare to the limits of safety, probably closer than humans ever have before, but only when we feel we are in control. When that protective framework is taken away, risk can switch to fear in an instant.

Chapter 6

Diversity, and

'Walk' would come on so I'd start across. Two seconds later 'Don't Walk' so I go back. Then on comes 'Walk' again. This went on for ten minutes: 'Walk. Don't Walk. Walk. Don't Walk.' I was practically out of my box. But what really stunned me was the way I just stayed there and obeyed the goddam machine for so long – I never even thought about going it alone. WILLIAM BOYD, *Not Yet, Jayette*

Conformity

Opportunity

Conformity in the city

In traditional society, life was relatively well ordered. People knew which group they belonged to and how each group related to other groups in the community. By contrast, the modern city appears to be a myriad of different people, looking distinctive and unalike. However, every public place in the city is governed by conventions of behaviour. Following these rules is essential if we are to be understood and accepted. In the crowded city, mass patterns of behaviour are forced upon us and form the fabric by which the city is bound.

Rules and laws To achieve the cohesion that is necessary in the complex world of city life, the behaviour of *homo urbanus* is governed by a host of rules. In some cases, these rules have become enshrined in laws and are subject to sanction.

Driving is perhaps one of our most regulated activities and, therefore, is a good example to consider. Our driving behaviour in most cities is carefully controlled and regulated by formal laws. We cannot drive on the wrong side of the road or go through red traffic lights. We are required to follow speed restrictions and stop at pedestrian crossings. At this level these laws are designed to protect us and others from danger, and tend to be accepted to some degree by most drivers. This is not to suggest we don't often break these laws. Most drivers will drive over the speed limit at some time and many will go through a traffic light as the light is changing to red. But to a large extent people tend to follow these laws and accept their general wisdom as safeguards.

> **STREET DANGERS AND OBEDIENCE**
>
> **I must absolutely pay attention to traffic laws, to lights and the traffic patterns. I once saw a man standing on the yellow line; he had himself trapped out there and I saw him get hit by the mirror, the side mirror of a passenger van. So things like that kind of make you obedient. There are Walk and Don't Walk signs that I had to figure out when I first moved here, and then you can time the lights: you have a certain amount of time to push the Don't Walk sign or something like that, but you really do have to pay attention to them.**
>
> JUDY – New York

Different laws have been designed with principles other than safety as their major objective. Parking restrictions typify these somewhat less accepted rules that have become laws. Where we can park a car, and for how long, are circumscribed and controlled. There are charges for parking in certain areas, and some places are reserved for specific activities such as loading or unloading vehicles. Breaking these rules may also lead to a formal sanction. Typically, in most cities, this is a fine. The frustrations of parking laws lead many people to ignore them and sanctions have been increased in many cities in an attempt to enforce observance. These now

Public places are governed by conventions which can be broken ...

... to assert one's individuality ...

... for example, by skating in the opposite direction.

include the infamous wheel clamp which immobilizes cars, and for some people, the even greater horror of having their car towed away to a car pound. Restrictions on parking are designed to prevent road blockages, to provide a parking turnover to give more people the opportunity to park, and also to restrict the number of cars coming into cities.

Controls on parking are accepted by most city dwellers as a fact of life, but for many the task is to get around these laws rather than follow them strictly. This illustrates the shift from laws to rules. Although there are formal laws about parking in most societies, they are embellished, altered, and reorganized by informal conventions or rules. These rules are sometimes accepted by most of the community but more often only by a small group.

In some cases, the authorities who control parking simply choose to ignore the breach of the written law. An example in London, where parking space is at a premium and private garages few, is that parking two abreast in the road is acceptable in certain streets at night.

In some cases, certain categories of drivers are judged to be able to break the laws. In parking it is acceptable for people who are on public duty or delivering goods to break parking laws.

In general, city dwellers follow these rules and are obedient to authority because we don't wish to risk the sanction of not doing so.

Conventions Besides these formal laws, there a number of conventions or rules about driving in cities. These rules are unwritten and often unspoken conventions about how we act as drivers. They are not subject to formal sanction and are not policed to ensure our obedience. They are normally embedded in a culture of driving in the city. As a result they differ between one city and another.

One example of such a convention in London is the notion of alternating between cars when two streams of traffic approach an obstruction. In

Traffic is highly regulated by formal laws as well as conventions. Nonetheless these are often flouted.

this situation it is generally accepted that cars should alternate, one coming from one lane followed by another coming from the second lane and so on. This rule, unwritten and unsanctioned, is generally well observed. The polite acceptance of a rule embodying equity and fairness tends to be taken on board by most rush hour drivers. In accommodating to this unspoken rule and providing access to the other car, drivers ensure a reasonable flow of traffic.

Other conventions to cope with the oddities of London streets have also grown and are generally accepted and relatively well regulated. In many of London's narrow streets, two-lane roads converge into a single lane and the two opposing streams of traffic have to confront each other. As streams of cars back up, it is accepted that one direction has access for a period of time and then the other stream is given an opportunity to move through. No traffic light or sign regulates this interaction. It is governed by tacit acceptance and life at the blockage appears to pass by without rancour. In other cities, where driving conventions are different, this implicit understanding does not work.

The importance of these conventions is that they oil the wheels of traffic flow. By accepting these rules, most drivers are able to achieve their objective of making the journey in the shortest possible time. This is, of course, an idealized view of these unspoken rules as they often get frayed at the edges, especially when there is an opportunity for one driver to gain some advantage by breaking the rules. While the offender may be subjected to anger and gesticulation, there are no laws about committing an offence, only social disapproval.

In addition, they make life somewhat more predictable for the driver than would otherwise be the case. Drivers can predict that at some time they will be able to enter the stream of traffic and although they give way to others, it is predictable that others will give way to them too.

Interpersonal behaviour We also have rules about interpersonal behaviour in the city. As was demonstrated in Chapter 3, the way in which we meet and interact with others in the city is different to what happens in the country. In the country, much more time is taken over normal exchanges than in the city, where we are often moving at some speed and limit the time we give to any interaction. Conventions regarding how we interact in the city are often governed by the twin needs of restricting ourselves from potential overload as well as coping with the speed of the city with its apparent enforced efficiency.

An example of this in the city is when driving and wishing to enter a queue of traffic we often indicate our intention by catching the eye of the relevant driver in the stream of traffic and at the same time, edging our car into the line. Similarly, when we wish to talk in a conversation we give off signals. One technique used is to turn our heads away from the speaker. This breaks off eye contact and provides a visual signal to the speaker. Gesticulating has a similar effect at indicating our desire to talk. At the auditory level, we may give a sharp intake of breath. Finally, just as we do when driving, we can push in. This we do verbally by raising our voice and talking through the other person.

Many of these behaviours governing our interactions with others are unconscious. The effect of having such conventions, however, is much the same as that governing our behaviour while driving. The rules can be broken without sanction but are designed to smooth our interactions. This becomes particularly important in the city where a great deal has to be done and complex negotiations conducted in often difficult and rushed circumstances. The efficiency with which we obey these conventions helps *homo urbanus* cope, adapt, and survive.

Local conventions   Some negotiations between people in cities enshrine more local conventions. To understand and act by these we have to know the rules. Negotiating our way around a city often brings this type of social convention sharply into focus.

In New York city, dealing with public transport is often highly pressurized. The pressure comes both from the density of people, but also from officials who assume a universal knowledge of the rules governing the interaction. Thus, to travel on a bus means you must have the correct change. A failure to appreciate this rule means being ignored. If the driver was to make an exception or deal with every deviation from the rule, the bus would be late and time delays are considered unacceptable. These kinds of rules are often learned in a particular city and culture and some people only realize that other cities are governed by different conventions when they travel.

Continuing the example of travelling on a bus, in some cities it is necessary to have bought a ticket before getting on the bus, in others it is necessary to purchase a ticket on entering the bus while in yet other cities, people sit down on the bus and then purchase a ticket. The number of these local city conventions governing our everyday behaviour is infinite. It is partly these local rules about all sorts of behaviour that gives each city its own particular personality and atmosphere.

Within the city too, different environments circumscribe behaviour in different ways. In some situations, the constraints are minimal and a whole range of miscellaneous behaviours are encouraged. In a city park, for instance, people can be found playing different ball games, walking, rollerblading or skating, picnicking and lying in the sun. There are few restrictions on people's activities and the essence of the environment is to provide that type of freedom.

Airports Out of necessity, the modern city has created certain environments where we are obliged to follow strict patterns of behaviour. These are often formal environments such as law courts, churches, libraries and theatres. One such situation which epitomizes the need to conform, and which is frequented by *homo urbanus*, is the airport.

Going to an airport is a common experience for many city dwellers. The average New Yorker and Londoner goes to airports more times a year than they go to art galleries. We all have a sequence in our heads, like a script, of what happens when we go through an airport for an international trip. The script goes something like this:

1   Arrive at airport
2   Scrutinize signs to see where to check in
3   Stand in line at the check-in counter
4   Check bags through and receive boarding card
5   Pass through to departures
6   Stand in line and show boarding card
7   Pass through airport security
6   Stand in line for bags to be X-rayed
7   Pass through security to passport control
8   Stand in line at passport control
9   Pass through passport control to shops and restaurants
10 Time to shop or eat
11 Go to gate for aircraft departure
12 Stand in line to show boarding pass and passport
13 Pass through and wait in holding area
14 Stand in line when boarding is announced
15 Board the aeroplane

AIRPORTS AND FLYING

You put yourself in their hands. They take complete charge, from the minute you give up your suitcase which has all your possessions in it, and you're physically checked; you're in their control, no doubt about it. I wouldn't have it otherwise. They've got your physical safety, your well-being in their hands, so you have to trust them.

ARTHUR – London

Waiting to pass through different points to be processed as a passenger characterizes the whole experience. Using an airport means following a clear set of signs and instructions and doing what people in uniform tell us to do. We quite literally cede control over our luggage and our persons to others and are ready to follow instructions. The whole process is rather like becoming an object that is checked and packaged for the aeroplane. The need for any individual decision making is severely constrained.

The pressure to conform does not end on boarding. During the flight, the air crew carefully cocoon passengers. They give out instructions, provide meals and show films, all of which serve to

In certain situations we have little choice and are obliged to follow a strict sequence of activities such as arriving at an airport for air travel

... checking in

... being channelled in one direction

... being ferried to departures

... passing through airport security

... waiting in a holding area

keep passengers calm and placid, not having to think independently. The new development of personal videos and video games has succeeded even further in keeping passengers firmly in their seats, making the job of transportation even easier. The situation encourages passengers to cede responsibility to the air crew so that in times of emergency they are more likely to obey instructions.

Although the regimen of routine on board can be intensive, it helps to create the illusion that nothing can go wrong, and when we have been rendered passive to the point of helplessness this can be very reassuring.

Bystander apathy Because the city is governed by conventions of behaviour, we are often unwilling to question the conviction of the majority. When, for example, we see someone lying on a busy city pavement where no one else is stopping, most people keep walking – an all too common event which can make the city appear a callous place. Fear and suspicion play their part, but most importantly we look to each other to judge how to behave. Only when one person has stopped to help do the rules of the situation change, allowing others to intervene.

The idea that the city is a sea of strangers has led to a view that cities are places where you cannot get help in times of trouble. A number of well-publicized studies, as well as incidences and crimes of assault, have fostered this view. Studies have shown that nearly 80 per cent of people feel that a person is more likely to get help from a stranger in a small town than in a city. In fact, the evidence suggests that there is only a relatively small grain of truth with this view. Some studies in the

... ceding responsibility to the air crew and lose our sense of individuality and control.

I don't like airports because they take away your control. You have no control over your life from the time you arrive until the time you depart. If you know nothing about flying or aviation I always think, when I'm on a plane, that there's nothing I could do in an emergency: that I would just have to trust the person who's in charge.

The passport control, them taking your luggage away from you, a certain time you have to board, a certain time you have to be seated. You can smoke at a certain time, you can stop smoking, you have to eat at a certain time, those sort of things make you in to a bit of a machine.

JOHN – New York

It stems from that period of vulnerability, that you're in a situation where you're totally out of control, you're in someone else's hands. I feel uneasy; you're put into an environment again where you don't have control, and from someone that usually controls his situation it's tough to deal with, it builds up that anxiety.

RICHARD – New York

BYSTANDER APATHY

I couldn't live with myself if I just walked away from something. It scares me because I think if I were really in trouble – God forbid I got stabbed and was laying in the street – I think people would walk right over me and go to where they were going, just for fear of not getting involved.

ERROL – Los Angeles

If you're going to talk about, let's say, somebody being homeless, and you talk about being desensitized, this is something that we see almost every day, and it's not something that is an out-of-place occurrence.

PEPSI – New York

You get a lot of beggars who sleep rough and sometimes it's difficult to tell whether somebody is ill or whether it's somebody just dossing. You can't always tell. And to some extent the city does make you a bit hard. If I actually saw somebody physically collapsing, yes, I would help, but as opposed to seeing somebody just lying on the street, I would tend to probably walk past, not get involved.

ARTHUR – London

USA have shown that cities with populations above 300,000 show a small decline in helping behaviour. What is important is that this is situationally defined. It is not that individuals who are city dwellers have developed a personality which is harsh and uncaring. Although helping behaviour declines in urban environments, city dwellers are as likely to offer help in rural environments and rural or small town dwellers less likely to help in urban environments.

Two theories, which have some common features, have been proposed as to why helping behaviour in urban environments is less than in non-urban environments. One theory suggests that the external demands on a city dweller cause overload which results in the screening out of stimuli that are not essential. By this view the city dweller does not process the information that somebody requires help. The second theory attributes the lack of helping behaviour to the fact that when someone is in a large group of people it is not clear who should take responsibility. By this process the diffusion of responsibility means that a person is not moved to action because it may not be seen as his or her responsibility.

Further studies in a large number of cities in the USA examined people's responses to different kinds of situations in which help may be expected. These included a blind person wanting to cross the street, asking for change and dropping a pen on the street amongst others. These studies found that population density as opposed to population size were predictive of all these forms of helping behaviour, and were particularly important in situations which required spontaneous helping behaviour as opposed to behaviour following a request. These findings provide support for both of the theories mentioned above.

The reality is that the decision to help a stranger in the city is a complex one, reached only after we take into account a number of factors in the situation. The most difficult and complex decisions are in situations where violence is a possibility. For instance, bystanders make a judgement about the threat of violence towards themselves which influences whether they intervene or not. Other forms of helping behaviour have more complex explanations. Research shows bystanders are influenced by the signals they pick up from situations.

In 1991, Harrison conducted a study which showed that strangers were more likely to offer assistance if they saw that a friend or associate of the person in danger was distressed or anxious about what was happening. People's reactions to an experimental situation were studied in which they were found to make an assessment before going to a victim's assistance. This assessment entailed judging whether a friend of the victim was perturbed or not by a scream and crash coming from a room into which the victim had gone. When the friend's behaviour was agitated, they were more likely to offer help than when it was not. These findings show that we use other people's behaviour to help us define what has happened and what we should do. The fact that we act in concert with others also allows us to share the responsibility.

Excitement and diversity in the city

People like the city because it offers them diverse opportunities and greater choice in their life. Research indicates that city dwellers believe the city offers a diverse set of activities, a wide choice of friends, an energetic lifestyle, greater freedom of expression, a great deal of entertainment and lifestyle choice. None of these things tend to be associated with small towns. It is this kaleidoscope of change and variety that captures one of the most attractive aspects of city living. It offers us a potential to choose those spaces and places that must express the way we are and want to behave.

In many large cities of North America and western Europe, it is possible to eat the cuisine of almost any other nation. In London, for example, within a fifteen-minute walking distance in the central district of Soho it is possible to sample the food of India, China, Indonesia, France, Korea, Vietnam, Thailand, Italy, Greece, Afghanistan, Turkey, Nepal, Spain, and Algeria. It is even possible to sample the food from different regions within countries: Szechwan in China or Kerala in India for instance. The number of different activities, be they sporting, social or recreational, in any big city, is more than can be accomplished by anyone. The city provides the means whereby we can satisfy a whole host of different interests, all clustered within a relatively small geographic area. The essence of most large cities is stimulation. They invigorate and arouse people. The city is the candlelight to moths, drawing us in to see or take part in everything on offer.

MOVING TO THE BIG CITY

In the town where I grew up there was one thing to do. One time of year there was a fair that was in town five days and you saved all your money, bought brand new clothes, and that was what you did from nine in the morning 'til twelve at night, and then it shut down, and for these five days it was great. But other than that there was a lot of times of trying to think of things to do. You pretty much knew what was going on every weekend; it was pretty routine.

When I came to the big city it was like I was a kid in a candy store. There was a million things to do every weekend.

DAVE – Los Angeles

Clothes as markers In the city, the use of dress as a non-verbal cue to convey information about the self is important.

When we are in public we are on view to other people and want to signal our social group, attitudes and personality to others. We want to create an impression of who we are. This enables us to make contact with like-minded people and avoid others whom we don't see as like-minded. Modes of dress are particularly important with regard to self presentation. Different groups often use clearly identifiable styles of dress and clothes to

Clothes, make-up, jewellery and hairstyle are very important in self-presentation and are a significant non-verbal marker about who we are and what we like.

be easily recognized. Using T-shirts and sweatshirts with clearly labelled identifiers of places visited or affiliations are ways in which we can identify ourselves and have a clear opener for social interaction with others.

The extent of our unconscious attitudes towards clothes as a sign of group membership has been demonstrated in the finding that we are more likely to follow the behaviour of somebody who is dressed like us. Studies in the United States show people are more likely to jaywalk after somebody has initiated jaywalking if they are dressed alike than if they are not dressed alike.

People who are part of a particular group tend to agree what clothes are suitable for which events.

None are more sensitive about the clothes they wear than adolescents. Clothes are the determining feature of whether a person is accepable to belong to the group. The age at which children are becoming interested in fashion has dropped, according to a recent report, to about ten years. The structure of clothes has changed in order to signal clearly which brand is being worn by placing the labels on the outside. This makes easy identification of fashion and price allowing someone to tell at a distance whether the individual is up with fashion and is a suitable person to associate with.

Besides clothes, make-up and in particular hairstyle are all part of the process of giving off signals as to our group. Hair has become an industry of self expression. The one aspect of our bodies that seems to be infinitely malleable is our hair. The way hair is worn in some traditional societies signals status and position. In the city, hairstyles also signal group membership. The industry of hairdressers seeking to create different styles serve to keep the fashion in a constant state of flux.

Some other signals of group membership are much more subtle and may involve small differences in behaviour. In England, where social grouping or class continues to make social distinctions, people's accent and the manner of speaking are all cues to our social group. These kinds of groupings tend to be more fixed than others, although the greater variety permitted in the city suggests that they are more likely to be secondary determinants of friendship and association.

Clothes are a sign of the social groups to which we belong or identify with.

Different roles In the fast-moving city we have to prepare ourselves for the various different situations we pass through. Many city dwellers move comfortably through a variety of roles within a day. A typical day in the life of *homo urbanus* might include going to the gym before breakfast, taking children to school, commuting to work, going to a lunchtime concert, having dinner with friends in a restaurant before moving on to the theatre. What is important is that the city offers all these alternative activities and the city dweller is expected to and succeeds in moving comfortably through a host of activities and roles within a short period of time. The ease with which it is possible to slip in and out of these roles is a skill most city dwellers have learned.

> ### THE ILLUSION OF INDIVIDUALITY
>
> **Actually, you end up reinventing yourself as one of many Guardian readers that all sit in their back gardens, and you look across and everybody's there on a Saturday morning reading their Guardian with a nice coffee percolating, and we're all doing exactly the same stuff. That was the kind of saddest moment, when I sat down and did literally that, and realized we're all individuals, and all exactly the same.**
>
> ALEX – London

Each role makes its own particular demands on our behaviour. As with group membership, style of dress indicates clearly to others our transition through different environments. Although some individuals try harder to ensure their clothes fit in with a particular group or activity, most people conform to some degree in the clothes they wear on different occasions. Some years ago these different forms of dress were formalized into dress codes, with one common distinction that is still maintained today – between formal and informal wear. But even with the introduction of less formality around clothes, people do tend to dress carefully for the occasion, often making important distinctions that individuals who are not part of the groups would miss.

Stereotypes Stereotypes are convenient shorthand ways for us to summarize a situation or people, because the city presents a fast-moving ever-changing environment. When we are overloaded, stereotypes lend themselves to making quick judgements about situations and people. They may not always be accurate and they can often be dangerously wrong, but they are used regularly in a relatively benign way in the city to make judgements and decisions. Likewise, the way an individual dresses or acts is very often aimed at putting across a particular image or stereotype of what they represent.

Passing someone on the way to work, we often summarize their social position and attitudes by briefly glancing at their dress, or maybe the car they are driving, or newspaper they are reading. The stereotypes we use offer a rapid way of summing up others or even different situations, without investing much energy or effort. To the extent that the people behave in the expected or predicted way, our stereotype is supported and continues to provide us with a shorthand for dealing with the wide diversity of city life.

Stereotypes do have an excluding effect. By using limited cues to provide us with a rapid opinion of other people we may choose to limit our interactions. We may decide not to go to certain places because we believe they will not offer something we enjoy. The problem with the shorthand of stereotypes is that they restrict experience. The dilemma for city dwellers is that they are overwhelmed by so much diversity that finding their way requires the use of some shorthand techniques.

Off-stage In a busy city we may think it is easy to ignore others, but in fact we are all acutely aware of the behaviour going on around us. But although we are all 'on stage', being observed by others, certain groups are more on stage than others. These are often people performing a service role where they are open to direct evaluation, and the quality of their job is in part determined by their public presentation.

Waiters in restaurants are an example of such a group. When they leave the kitchen they must adopt a particular pose and often carefully crafted solicitous behaviour. Although the kitchen is not a strictly private place, it enables them to step off the stage of the restaurant and fall back on behaviour which is more natural.

And although the restaurant's lavatory is still a semi-public place, here we know that we can behave in front of each other in a way that would not be tolerated by the other diners. We are free to adjust our clothing without embarrassment, to preen ourselves before returning to the more formal atmosphere of the dining room. City dwellers draw upon a range of known rules and observed behaviour that tells them what is required.

Using public space Different places in most large cities cater for different interests. In one part of the city certain clubs may be grouped; in another, particular types of shops may be located. We frequently pass from one area to another in the city, from street corner to street corner, each full of diversity; different people with different affiliations and interests. People with specific interests often tend to group around a particular building, shop or pub, although this may not be obvious until the building is entered. For example, although public places, London pubs often specifically cater for particular groups such as gay men, young people, or punks. Similarly, singles bars in New York might only be identifiable as such from the inside. *Homo urbanus* has an acute ability to sum up situations and environments from a limited set of social cues.

Certain public environments are occupied by particular groups of people. City squares are often colonized and become associated with different groups. Notable amongst the new breed of colonizers are bicycle and motorcycle messengers. Using their radios they often congregate in specific places of the city to await the next order. Public spaces can have different occupants at different times of the day or week. During lunch periods office workers are on the move and in good weather chase the sun in the squares. In certain areas, older residents may make more use than others of a square.

Subverting the rules   Knowing the rules of how to behave, especially in formalized situations, can have surprising advantages. By observing the rules we can subvert them to suit ourselves. Some public spaces in the city are taken over and used for purposes other than those for which they were intended. For example, part of the outdoor parking areas in one of London's theatre complexes has been co-opted by skateboarders as it offered a useful camber to perform turns and jumps.

In other situations, the area continues to perform its intended function at the same time as being used for other purposes. In many cities, the supermarket has become a place to meet people of a similar age or sexual preference. In some cases, shopping is done by different groups on different evenings. One night may be for gay men, another for over thirties. The rules are implicit, and what makes them interesting is how these informal groupings develop and how information about them spreads. Most people going to these shops continue to do their shopping but also have the opportunity to meet others.

Freedom and flexibility

Movement between worlds in the city As we have shown, the city allows us to sample many worlds every day. We not only look at the worlds of others but often are able to experience different worlds as well. This provides the city dweller with seemingly infinite choices from which to sample what they do. It also provides a sense of freedom and liberation as well as excitement. Because there is so much diversity, city dwellers feel that they can do what they want and are not tied to a strict code of behaviour. Many cities are characterized by tolerance and acceptance of difference. For some, this may reflect a lack of interest or concern, but for others it is one of the attractive aspects of city life. This sense of freedom and liberation is certainly true in contrast to rural life. The city offers a range of different alternative norms and rules to guide our behaviour.

What is important is that the city is responsive to innovations and to trying out new things that have not been done before. Some people in the city continually attempt to test the norms or rules of different environments. Most cities are extremely tolerant about differences and they may lead to new forms of behaviour. There are countless examples of new ways of behaving being introduced into cities. Jogging on city streets was almost unheard of twenty years ago. Rollerblading to work along Manhattan streets is a new phenomena. It is the dynamism of the city and its flexibility that are appealing to many city dwellers.

Rollerblading provides one way of beating the traffic. We can be both unconventional and assert our identity.

You can actually be just about whatever, legally, you want to be. You only have to walk down one or two streets to see people. Dress and style is always the first thing obviously you notice about people, and anything goes, really virtually anything goes.

ANASTASIA – London

This is the city, it is the place you can come and have a nervous breakdown and get it all out of your system, and go completely crazy and nobody would even arrest you. They wouldn't stop you, they wouldn't even look at you wrong.

JODIE – Los Angeles

I feel that the city allows you to be yourself and express yourself. Basically you have every type of nationality, every race, every creed in the city, one place or another. As there's so much variety I find that you get used to seeing a lot of that, so when someone wants to be unique and to be an individual, it's a lot easier . . . if you were [in] a small town and didn't have much variety, if you're different in the least bit, it attracts so much attention, so much scrutiny, and it's much more difficult, even if you are a strong individual.

PEPSI – New York

London's got so much to offer. Whatever you're interested in, London basically has it. Whatever your interests, you can definitely find it in London. You can express yourself and grow and develop as a person in whichever way you choose to . . .

ARTHUR – London

You can be yourself, because you're anonymous at many times of the day. You can go out and be completely lost in a crowd, whereas in a village, for example, or where people know you, you're very much somebody who everybody else knows and somebody else has got preconceived ideas about. You can re-invent yourself in a city, completely re-invent yourself.

ALEX – London

There's the freedom of the city to express yourself in different various forms, specially clothes and your appearance. Nobody looks twice at you whereas I suppose in a village if you had pink hair or something then people's attention is more drawn to you. So it allows you that freedom.

JANE – London

The city offers a range of different norms and rules. It is the flexibility and the dynamism of the city and that is appealing.

The tolerance, freedom and diversity of the city creates a crucible for change. New ideas and attitudes evolve, old conformities and values are challenged and replaced. The dynamism of the city is addictive and continues to exert its compelling attraction. And human beings will always take up the city's challenges, changing and adapting to the urban environment in an ever-evolving process.

CITY AND DIVERSITY

New York City is the big place where everything happens. There's all kinds of people here. I was looking around, I think, when I came to New York. But I was like, wow, everything's here. All these tall, big business-like looking people, from them to people who were pushing cards, delivering stuff, there's just a million things going on at once.

JOHN – New York

If I hadn't been born here I would have ended up here. I just desire this activity and the whole myriad of possibilities.

RICHARD – New York